Instant Pot® VEGETARIAN COOKBOOK

Instant Pot®
VEGETARIAN COOKBOOK

Fast & Healthy Recipes for Your Favorite Electric Pressure Cooker

SRIVIDHYA GOPALAKRISHNAN

Photography by Nadine Greeff

ROCKRIDGE
PRESS

To my son, Raghav, little sous chef.

To my husband, Manikandan,
my pillar of strength and my critic.

To my mom, my cooking guru.

To my family and to my readers.

And to my dad, whose loving memory
has guided me in this endeavor.

Contents

Interior and Cover Designer: Darren Samuel
Photo Art Director: Sue Smith
Editor: Carolyn Abate
Production Editor: Erum Khan
Photography © 2018 Nadine Greeff
Cover recipe: Ratatouille, page 69

ISBN: Print 978-1-64152-422-3 | eBook 978-1-64152-423-0

Introduction

I remember the very first dish I cooked for my family when I was 13. It was *upma*, a thick, savory porridge made with semolina. My mom introduced me to day-to-day cooking as soon as I entered my teens. I'm grateful because it taught me to be independent and responsible.

It also made me fall in love with vegetables, fruits, and spices—I grew up eating only vegetarian meals. Most of all, spending time with my mom in the kitchen made me fall in love with cooking. I learned that the way to reach the heart is through food. With my family's encouragement, I tried new recipes and enjoyed experimenting in the kitchen. Cooking and feeding the people I love gave me immense satisfaction.

When I moved to the States as an adult, I was introduced to other cuisines: classic American, Italian, Caribbean, Ethiopian, Thai, Mexican, and Mediterranean. My joy knew no bounds. I loved it all! I learned new recipes and created vegetarian versions for myself. I started my blog, *Vidhya's Vegetarian Kitchen*, to document my mother's recipes, but soon I began sharing my take on vegetarian recipes from around the world.

I've always used a pressure cooker to create meals. In India, many home cooks turn to stove top pressure cooking time and again to create delicious meals. When I came to the United States, I duly packed my own.

When I got my first Instant Pot® in 2015, I was intrigued. It offered so many more functionalities than my standard stove-top pressure cooker. I didn't have to constantly hover over it and worry about burning myself when releasing pressure. What's more, it has preset buttons and a host of functionalities not found on my traditional pressure cooker. From sautéing and steaming to baking and pressure cooking, you can do it all in the Instant Pot®.

It's no exaggeration to say that I love my 6-quart DUO Instant Pot®. So much so that I bought a companion for it: the LUX Mini. Both are essential in my kitchen. My mini even comes with us when we camp or take road trips. It doesn't take up much space, making it so easy to whip up healthy meals for my family of three wherever we may be.

My recipes are a reflection of my passions for vegetarian cooking and the Instant Pot®. I've created easy, delicious, healthy vegetarian recipes with readily available ingredients. In this book, you'll find everything from classic dishes such as Baked Beans (page 44) and Minestrone (page 67) to more adventurous recipes like Mixed-Vegetable Korma (page 32) and Savory Rice Porridge (page 99). I encourage you to try it all.

Chapter One
MEATLESS MADE EFFORTLESS

When you hear "meatless meals," what comes to mind? You may think of a vegetable stir-fry, while others may envision lentil soup. Lucky for us, today's modern vegetarian cooking means many things to many people.

However you define meatless meals, I've got you covered. You won't have to spend a lot of time preparing my recipes. With the Instant Pot®, it's now easy to make delicious, well-balanced vegetarian meals in no time. That's the beauty of the Instant Pot®—effortless, efficient cooking. From salads and soups to curries and desserts, you can make it all in the Instant Pot®.

INSTANT POT® 101

If you are new to Instant Pot® cooking, welcome! (If you already own an Instant Pot® and are familiar with its benefits, feel free to skip ahead to the next section.) Let me offer a quick run-down of the Instant Pot® and why it's so popular.

At its core, the Instant Pot® is a smart, programmable multi-cooker. It includes the functionality of a multitude of cooking modes and methods: It can sauté, pressure cook, slow cook, steam, and sterilize—all in the same vessel. It also acts as a warmer. You can make yogurt, rice, soup, or stews. The list goes on and on.

Unlike the pressure cookers of yore, the Instant Pot® doesn't require you to babysit it. While it works its cooking magic, you can hang out in the kitchen or catch up on some reading or whatever you have to do. The timer lets you know when cooking has finished. Even then, it automatically moves into Keep Warm mode. It's stress-free cooking at its finest.

Most people turn to the Instant Pot® because of its pressure cooking capabilities. The term "pressure cooking" simply refers to the process of using liquid in a sealed vessel to cook food. When heated, the liquid inside begins to boil. The sealed pot traps in all of the steam from the boiling process. This causes the internal pressure and temperature to rise at a very fast rate, cooking the ingredients very quickly.

Instant Pot® Benefits

The Instant Pot® uses the same pressure cooking engineering and mechanics as stove top models, but it also provides some additional—and significant—advantages.

Speed. Compared to traditional stove top cooking, the Instant Pot® can cut cooking time by as much as 75 percent. For example, beans cooked on a stove top range from 40 minutes to 3 hours. The Instant Pot® cuts those cook times by one-third to one-half, depending on the type of bean and whether you presoaked them.

Ease and Convenience. With the simple press of a button, the machine can preheat itself and automatically switch to the cook setting you've selected. Once finished, it then automatically switches to the Keep Warm setting. Another convenience is quick pressure release, which allows for fine control on cooking time, creating perfectly finished meals.

Energy Savings. The speed of the Instant Pot® makes it energy efficient. Shorter cooking time directly translates to using less energy. The Instant Pot® also uses less water compared to stove top boiling or steaming; most vegetable recipes call for just 1 cup of water to steam.

Safety. Traditional stove-top pressure cookers come with a safety hazard—they sometimes explode if the heat isn't turned off at the right time. The Instant Pot® eliminates this safety concern because it goes directly to the Keep Warm mode after cooking.

Nutrition. Instant Pot® cooking methods retain up to 90 percent of the vitamins and minerals in foods compared to regular stove top cooking.

Cleaning. It is easy to clean and maintain your Instant Pot®. You can remove the tough grease with some white vinegar and gentle soap solution.

VEGETARIAN THE INSTANT POT® WAY

Whether you're preparing a weeknight dinner for two or a weekend dinner party for twelve, most Instant Pot® recipes call for the same cooking steps. The good news is they aren't complicated and usually warrant only the push of a button.

1. Precooking ingredients. Not all recipes call for precooking, but if one does, it usually involves sautéing. For example, Vegetable Jambalaya (page 84) requires that you first sauté the onions and vegetables before adding the other ingredients. I prepared all these recipes in the DUO model. While the DUO mode uses Less, Normal, and More heat settings, the new Ultra model has different names for these: Low, Medium, and High. The Ultra model also allows you to set custom temperature. If you are using an Ultra, you can use the Medium heat setting as the default. If a recipe calls for More, like French Onion Soup (page 63) or Vegetable Lo Mein (page 95), then you can select the High.

2. Adding liquid. Most recipes call for a liquid such as water or broth. It's also important to add a sufficient amount of liquid based on the size of your Instant Pot®. When steaming vegetables in a steaming basking, first add the water to the Instant Pot®. Place the trivet in the pot, then the steamer basket on top of that. For vegetables cooked in larger pieces, such as butternut squash, place the larger piece directly on the trivet. Use the same steps when using stacking pans. For beans, add them first and then add the needed water to the inner pot.

To Use or Not to Use Presets

The Instant Pot®'s front panel has settings for Slow Cook, Sauté, and Pressure Cooking. Depending on your Instant Pot® model, it may also come with preset cook times for various ingredients, including Rice, Bean, Multigrain, Porridge, and Yogurt.

Presets are especially useful for helping beginners understand cooking duration patterns. You don't have to think about cooking on Low or High pressure modes. They're also designed to deliver consistent results.

So if presets are worry-free, why would anyone choose the Pressure Cook or Manual setting? I use it for recipes with special ingredients, such as fava beans, tofu, and noodles, to ensure they aren't overcooked. I also use Manual mode when making smaller amounts of certain recipes such as Curried Carrot and Ginger Soup (page 60) or Cilantro-Lime Rice (page 79).

Manual mode accommodates individual tastes, too. I find the Rice preset always delivers perfectly cooked rice, but when my mom visits, I cook rice in the Manual setting because she likes it very soft.

In some models, the Pressure Cook or Manual selections allow you to set cook time and pressure level (High or Low). The Instant Pot® begins its countdown when pressure is reached. After cooking, the device lets you know when it's finished. You then release the pressure either naturally or quickly.

With the Steam mode, you can steam or reheat food. There are a number of steps you must take before you begin Steam mode (see "Adding liquid" on page 3). You must also make sure you've added a sufficient amount of water to the vessel.

3. Locking the lid into place. It's crucial that, before you begin pressure cooking, the steam release knob is in the sealed position. If it's not, the pot won't build pressure.

4. Selecting the setting, adjusting pressure, and indicating the cooking time. If you're using a preset functionality, press the appropriate button when you're ready to cook. To cook in Pressure Cook or Manual, set the pressure level (High or Low), then enter the cook time. Note: Not every model has a Start button. Some displays will change to ON after you set the cook time. The cooking begins 10 seconds after that. Initially, you may hear a soft sound; this is the machine building pressure. If the sound is loud, make sure the steam release knob is in the sealed position.

5. Releasing pressure. After cooking, release the pressure per the recipe's instructions. To quick release, press Cancel and move the steam release knob to the Vent position. (Some models will also have a steam release button that needs to be pressed after moving the knob.) To release naturally, press Cancel and wait for the pressure to come down on its own—usually 15 to 20 minutes. Some recipes call for natural release and then quick release. If that's the case, let the pressure release naturally for the specific amount of time, then move the steam release knob to the Vent position to quick release the remaining pressure.

VEGETARIAN UNDER PRESSURE

Pressure cooking is a convenient, efficient way to prepare vegetarian dishes. However, different ingredients call for different pressure modes, cooking methods, and cook times. It's important to understand which ingredients cook best at Low pressure, High pressure, and even in Sauté mode.

In general, vegetables cut into large chunks can tolerate high-pressure cooking; smaller chunks cannot. The vegetable itself also plays a major role. Root vegetables, such as carrots, potatoes, and beets, are perfect for high-pressure cooking because their high starch content can endure intense heat. Vegetables with a high water content are finicky. Tomatoes, cauliflower, and broccoli quickly turn to mush if left just a minute too long.

Cooking grains and beans is fairly straightforward, although cook times are determined by the quality and variety of bean and whether they're soaked overnight. For Hummus (page 36), I cook chickpeas until they are very soft, as they'll be puréed. For Chickpea Greek Salad (page 37), I prefer that they retain their form, so I cook them for less time.

Water also plays a major role when it comes to appropriately cooked grains, especially rice. In my Za'atar-Spiced Bulgur Wheat Salad (page 106) and Couscous Pilaf (page 100), I opt for cook times and water that produce non-sticky, tender grains. For my Apple-Cinnamon Oat Porridge (page 98), I always add a little extra water and cook for a longer time to get a creamy consistency.

If you have excess water after cooking grains, you can simply drain it off before serving.

Foods to Cook

The Instant Pot® is terrific for all types of dishes—soups, stews, main dishes, side dishes, and even desserts. They can all be made in an Instant Pot® because of the different functionalities the machine offers.

Soups and stews, in particular, are perfect to make in the Instant Pot®. The machine cuts their cook times in half, and you don't even have to transfer them to serving bowls—simply serve from the Instant Pot®.

Dishes that call for grains, beans, and lentils work really well in the Instant Pot® because you can either use the preset functions or cook them on Pressure Cook or Manual and at High or Low pressure. A lot of that is really up to your personal preference.

You'll also see that I don't shy away from using a variety of vegetables in my dishes. It's true that sturdy vegetables, such as beets or potatoes, hold up well under pressure cooking. But I use a lot of delicate vegetables as well, such as button mushrooms, bok choy, and spinach. When dishes call for high–water content vegetables, I usually sauté them first to bring out their flavor.

Desserts also get the full Instant Pot® treatment in my house. I use the machine to make cakes and yogurt. I even proof bread in it! Simply turn on the yogurt setting at Low temperature for perfectly proofed bread every time.

Foods to Avoid

While almost any food can be cooked in an Instant Pot®, some do have their challenges. Dairy-based recipes need special attention because they can quickly curdle. When a recipe calls for a dairy ingredient, I usually turn off the Instant Pot® and set it to Keep Warm, then add the ingredient. I also don't bake bread or cookies in the Instant Pot®. Both need space to rise and expand, and the Instant Pot® doesn't offer that.

Understanding Pressure Levels

Understanding how the Instant Pot® works requires some basic understanding of boiling point temperatures and pressure levels (psi, or pounds per square inch). In a sealed pot such as the Instant Pot®, the boiling point of water increases as the pressure rises. With the Duo Instant Pot® model, High pressure varies between 10.2 and 11.6 psi, so water's boiling point ranges between 239°F and 242°F. Low pressure ranges from 5.8 to 7.2 psi, so water's boiling point ranges between 212°F and 223°F.

Most Instant Pot® recipes call for cooking with High pressure. If a recipe calls for Low pressure, you can always cook in High mode for a shorter length of time. (This is especially important for models, like the LUX, that only have High pressure mode.) A rice recipe that cooks at Low for 12 minutes can be cooked instead for 6 minutes on High. Pressure is then released naturally for 10 minutes before quick releasing any remaining pressure (see Top Tips for Instant Pot® Success, Natural or quick pressure release, page 11). When it comes to vegetables, always cook for a shorter time, even 0 minutes. When you choose 0 minutes as the cooking time, the pressure builds up and then it automatically goes to Keep Warm.

Pressure decreases with increasing altitude. With the new Ultra model, you can adjust the altitude as well. However, if you are using a DUO model and living in a high altitude area, increase the cooking time by 5 percent for every 1,000 feet above 2,000 feet elevation.

CREATING VEGETARIAN MEALS

Maintaining a healthy vegetarian diet means eating well-balanced meals with the right ratio of carbs, proteins, fat, and vitamins and minerals. That is my guiding principle when I'm developing recipes. My Thai-Style Vegetable Curry (page 30) is loaded with vegetables and tofu, and I love serving it with brown rice and Green Bean Stir-Fry (page 21). My Minestrone (page 67) features vegetables and lentils; serve it with some rustic French bread, and you've got a perfect meal. The key is good planning.

All About Flavor

Pressure cooking does a superb job of bringing out the intense flavors of food. Start off with the right amount of seasoning and spice, and let the steam do its work.

Basics to Build Flavor

Here are some techniques I turn to when cooking in my Instant Pot®. I usually begin with a small amount of seasoning and adjust accordingly. It's all about finding your preference.

- For smoky flavors, add cumin, ground coriander, or smoked paprika. Together or separately, they add depth to any dish.

- For a different take on sweetness, I like to use cardamom seeds, cinnamon, and allspice, which also offers earthy flavors.

- Vegetable broth is an excellent addition for increasing flavor, especially when cooking rice or beans.

- Acid helps sharpen flavors. Lemon juice, citrus zest, apple cider vinegar, and balsamic vinegar are just a few examples.

- Build umami, or salty flavor, with ingredients such as soy sauce, miso, olives, capers, sun-dried tomatoes, and mushrooms. Be sure to reduce the amount of salt if you add any of these ingredients to your recipe.

- Adding sugar to savory dishes balances out the saltiness and sourness without reducing the amount of acid and umami. That's why most Thai dishes call for small amounts of cane sugar or honey.

Batch Cooking Bliss

Getting dinner on the table during busy weeknights is challenging. All too often, many of us end up throwing something together haphazardly—think hastily made grilled cheese or plain pasta. But with the Instant Pot®, meal planning is a breeze.

Spending a little time on the weekend to batch cook some staple items can alleviate week-night cooking headaches. On the weekends, I make all my sauces and steam a bunch of sturdy vegetables, such as beets and Brussels sprouts. I also cook batches of beans, rice, and quinoa. With those ready and available, I have endless meal options during the busy week:

- Grain bowls with quinoa, beans, and steamed vegetables

- Tacos with beans, rice, cheese, onions, and stir-fried vegetables

- Chinese–style noodle soups with steamed veggies and soy sauce

- Vegetarian stews with quinoa, beans, and steamed vegetables

- Enchilada casserole with beans and cheese

Thanks to the Instant Pot®, it's easy to prep ahead and take away the hassle of planning healthy weekday meals.

THE VEGETARIAN INSTANT POT® PANTRY

A well-stocked pantry is the key to meal prep success. From grains and beans to vegetables, spices, and more, here are some of my favorite ingredients:

Grains. Carbohydrates provide energy that your body needs, plus the added benefit of fiber. I always have on hand whole grains such as brown rice, bulgur wheat, millet, oats, and quinoa, in addition to couscous and pasta.

Beans and Legumes. Since they are the primary sources of protein for vegetarians, I stock different bean and legume varieties to keep meals interesting. This includes black beans, black-eyed peas, cannellini beans, chickpeas, fava beans, lima beans, kidney beans, and pinto beans. Lentils are big in Indian cooking, so I always have red, yellow, and green varieties on hand.

Fruits and Vegetables. Fruits and vegetables add essential vitamins, minerals, and fiber to your diet. I make every effort to buy seasonally for peak flavor. It also keeps costs down. My go-tos include asparagus, beets, bell peppers, cabbage, carrots, cucumbers, squash, and, of course, leafy greens.

Spices and Herbs. Fresh herbs such as basil, cilantro, mint, oregano, parsley, and rosemary add a big flavor boost to any recipe. Basil, oregano, and thyme are good dried herbs to have around. I also turn to allspice, nutmeg, paprika, and black pepper for complex flavor and aroma.

Nuts and Oils. Nuts add healthy fat, plus extra crunch, to any dish. I keep on hand almonds, peanuts, and walnuts. Nut butters are perfect for smoothies, oatmeal, and some Asian-inspired dishes. High-quality extra-virgin olive oil and corn oil are also two good choices. I use avocado, coconut, and peanut oils, too, depending on the recipe.

Dairy. I always have on hand butter, heavy cream, milk, sour cream, and yogurt. You'll also find Cheddar, mozzarella, and Parmesan cheese in my refrigerator.

Specialty Items. When a recipe needs that something extra to bring out flavor, I turn to coriander seeds, cloves, cumin seeds, coconut milk, rice vinegar, soy sauce, and Sriracha sauce.

SUPPORTING EQUIPMENT

The Instant Pot® is an addictive piece of kitchen equipment. Add on a few supporting accessories, and you'll find it even harder to go back to your old ways of cooking. All of these are available for 3-, 6-, and 8-quart Instant Pots®.

Steamer Rack. This is essential for cooking vegetables. With correct timing, a steamer rack prevents vegetables from getting too soft.

Extra Sealing Rings. Investing in a handful of these will save you flavor headaches down the road. Because sealing rings absorb the flavor of every dish you cook—even after cleaning—I keep three on hand: one for sweet dishes; one for curries, soups, and stews; and one for whole grains.

Springform Pan. This is ideal for making quiche, casseroles, cheesecake, and cakes. The pan's handy buckle makes it easy to remove finished foods from the vessel.

Stacking Pans. These are my go-to accessories because you can cook two different dishes in one shot—just make sure the ingredients have similar cooking times. The pans are also ideal for reheating food.

Immersion Blender. When I make my Tomato-Basil Soup (page 58) or Beet Soup (page 59), I use my immersion blender. It creates the perfect consistency and keeps the dish a one-pot wonder.

Top Tips for Instant Pot® Success

Here are my top tips for cooking with the Instant Pot®:

Make sure there's enough liquid. Liquid plays a crucial role in pressure cooking. Always use at least 1 cup (water or broth), no matter what you're cooking. The liquid helps to build the pressure inside the pot; if there isn't enough, the food will burn.

Learn when to use natural or quick pressure release. Natural pressure release works best for sturdy ingredients such as grains and beans. For delicate items such as pasta or certain vegetables, quick pressure release better retains the food structure and texture.

Deglaze the pot. This usually occurs after you've sautéed ingredients but before you begin pressure cooking. Just add the liquid and scrape the browned bits from the bottom of the pot. This technique adds more flavor to the final dish.

Embrace the pot-in-pot (or PIP) method. Simply put, this involves placing one pot in the inner pot. Use stacking pans, springform pans, jars, and ramekins to follow the PIP method. Add water to the inner pot, then place the trivet inside. Place the vessel you're using on the trivet. If you're making a cake or casserole, be sure to cover the ingredients with aluminum foil so the condensed water doesn't get inside.

Cook tender ingredients for zero minutes. Setting the time to 0 minutes means you can easily cook vegetables without losing texture and color. Select the Steam or Manual option and set the time to 0. The Instant Pot® will get up to full pressure, then immediately switch to the Keep Warm mode.

SCALING RECIPES UP AND DOWN

Most recipes in this book make 4 to 8 servings. If you need to make a smaller amount or want to make a big batch for a party, it's important to know how to scale a recipe up or down—especially when it comes to the Instant Pot®.

Scaling Down

Scale down a recipe by cutting back on the ingredients. To scale down a recipe by half, you simply cut the ingredients in half—but not the cooking time. For example, cooking 1 cup or ½ cup of chickpeas take 30 minutes on High.

Pay particular attention to the amount of liquid in relation to the other ingredients and what you're making. Also remember to use only the minimum amount of liquid needed to build the pressure.

- When you cook chickpeas directly in the Instant Pot®, you need to add 1 cup of water whether you have 1 cup, ½ cup, or ¼ cup of chickpeas.

- If a soup recipe calls for 4 cups of liquid and you scale it down to one-quarter of the recipe, the liquid should be reduced to 1 cup. However, if the ingredients aren't immersed in the liquid, add ½ cup more.

- To scale down a recipe for rice or quinoa, use the PIP method. Pour the grain and the liquid into a separate baking dish or pot and cover it tightly with foil. Then, add 1 cup of water to the Instant Pot®, place the trivet inside, and place the covered dish or pot with grains and water on top of that.

Scaling Up

It's easy to double or triple recipes. Simply make sure the liquid is also doubled or tripled. Here, the cooking time usually won't change, either. However, a doubled recipe that is using the PIP method doesn't need double the water in the inner pot of the Instant Pot®.

The size of your Instant Pot® also plays a role in how you scale up your recipes. Be sure to fill your Instant Pot® no more than two-thirds full; otherwise, the ingredients will spill over as it heats up.

When you double or triple a recipe, also never quick release the pressure. There's a good chance the food will splatter. Let pressure release naturally for at least for 5 minutes before doing a quick release.

INSTANT POT® TROUBLESHOOTING

Here are solutions to some of the most common Instant Pot® problems:

It's been 20 minutes, and pressure cooking hasn't started. Make sure the steam release knob is in the sealed position. Also check the sealing ring condition. If it's damaged, that could be another reason the pot won't cook.

Why did I get a Burn warning? The Burn warning is a new feature of more recent models. It is triggered when there isn't enough liquid and pressure doesn't build. If you get a Burn notice, add more liquid to deglaze the pot, scraping up any browned bits from the bottom, and then restart the cooking cycle. If the ingredients are fully scorched, empty the contents, clean the pot, and start all over.

My pudding smells like curry. The sealing ring absorbs all flavors you cook, so it's important to clean the ring after each use. Even better: Have separate rings for savory and sweet recipes.

My steam release knob is clogged. If you use too much liquid, your recipe will become frothy, which can clog the steam release knob. If the knob is clogged, remove the anti-shield block, carefully clean it, and place it back in the Instant Pot®.

My food is always dry or overcooked. After cooking, the Instant Pot® moves to Keep Warm mode, which can cause ingredients to dry out and overcook. I prefer to unplug the Instant Pot® rather than use the Keep Warm mode. When I'm ready to serve, I press Keep Warm.

The float valve isn't rising. Food particles sometimes get released during the cooking process and collect on the float valve, which prevents it from rising. If stuck, remove it from the lid, thoroughly clean it, and reattach. Check to see if the silicone cap is damaged, and replace it if necessary.

I can't open or close the lid. This occurs if the sealing ring isn't property set. Simply, unlock and remove the lid after the floating valve drops. Move the steam release knob to Vent, and when the pressure completely drops, open the lid.

The Skinny on the Mini

The Instant Pot® Mini is an excellent addition to your kitchen. This 3-quart model is the perfect companion to your 6- or 8-quart Instant Pot®. The compact size makes it ideal for small families. My Mini even comes with me every time we take a road trip.

The Mini comes in both LUX and DUO models. The Mini DUO includes a low-pressure yogurt option. If you want to make homemade yogurt or want to quickly proof your bread, then I recommend the Mini DUO. If you are buying it as a companion for your existing model, either option will do.

The main advantage with the Mini is its faster cooking time, because pressure rises more quickly compared to the larger models. The Mini also yields pretty reasonable portion sizes. It holds up to 2 cups of uncooked beans and 4 cups of uncooked rice, making a meal for up to four people possible. You can also use the PIP method with the Mini.

LET'S GET COOKING

I am excited for you to start trying my recipes. Most of the recipes have a preparation time of 10 minutes or less, but don't worry—even the recipes with longer prep times don't have complicated steps. The total cooking time noted in each recipe includes the roughly 10 minutes it takes for the Instant Pot® to come to pressure.

I created most of the recipes so they only use the Instant Pot® and don't require stove top cooking or oven roasting or baking steps. Just a few call for a blender or immersion blender for puréeing and making pastes.

Most of the recipes are gluten-free, and I have also provided vegan options. Many of the recipes are dairy-free and/or nut-free, too. Even better, you can easily swap some ingredients and make the recipes according to your preference. All the desserts are eggless.

Tips throughout the recipes will:

- Suggest ways to avoid waste by using ingredients in multiple recipes

- Describe how to increase or decrease the yield of a recipe

- Suggest recipes that pair well together

- Suggest ways to reinvent leftovers for fresh meals

Finally, a few notes on ingredients:

- Always adjust the salt and spices according to your preference.

- If using store-bought vegetable broth, adjust the salt you add according to the broth's sodium content. The same is true when using salted or unsalted butter.

- I prefer a neutral oil, such as corn oil, when I cook, so most of the recipes call for that. Feel free to swap in your favorite oil instead.

- If you forgot to soak the beans, increase the beans' cooking time by 8 to 10 minutes. Just make sure you rinse the beans thoroughly before cooking them.

I hope you enjoy the recipes as much as I enjoyed creating them!

Brussels Sprouts with Balsamic Vinegar

PAGE 22

Chapter Two
VEGETABLES AND SIDES

SPINACH-ARTICHOKE DIP

GLUTEN-FREE, NUT-FREE

SERVES 8

PREP AND FINISHING: 20 MINUTES

SAUTÉ: 5 MINUTES

PRESSURE COOK:
7 MINUTES ON HIGH

RELEASE: QUICK

TOTAL TIME: 40 MINUTES

INGREDIENT TIP: INSTEAD OF FRESH SPINACH, YOU CAN USE ABOUT 5 OUNCES (¾ CUP) FROZEN SPINACH, WHICH IS LESS EXPENSIVE. BE SURE TO THAW THE SPINACH TO ROOM TEMPERATURE BEFORE USING. COOK TIME AND PRESSURE REMAIN THE SAME WHEN THAWED.

Per Serving
Calories: 132; Fat: 11g;
Carbohydrates: 6g;
Fiber: 2g; Protein: 4g;
Sodium: 407mg

This creamy Spinach-Artichoke Dip is perfect for parties and get-togethers. If by chance some leftover dip remains after a gathering, it can also be used as a sauce for pastas or a spread for sandwiches. This dip is also perfect for making in bulk because it stores well in the refrigerator and freezer.

2 teaspoons corn oil

¼ cup chopped onion

2 garlic cloves, finely chopped

8 ounces fresh spinach, roughly chopped (about 1 bunch)

½ teaspoon kosher salt

1 teaspoon freshly ground black pepper

5 ounces cream cheese

1 (8½-ounce) can water-packed artichoke hearts, drained and quartered

⅓ cup heavy (whipping) cream

⅓ cup water

Chips or sliced veggies, for serving

1. Sauté the spinach. Select Sauté, and pour the oil into the inner pot. Once hot, add the onion and garlic and sauté for 1 minute. Add the spinach, salt, and pepper. Continue to sauté for 2 to 3 minutes or until the spinach is wilted. Add the cream cheese, artichokes, cream, and water and mix thoroughly.

2. Pressure cook the dip. Lock the lid into place. Select Pressure Cook or Manual, and adjust the pressure to High and the time to 7 minutes. Make sure the steam release knob is in the sealed position. After cooking, quick release the pressure.

3. Serve the dip. Unlock and remove the lid. Stir the dip, then leave it to cool in the Instant Pot® with the lid off. Transfer to a serving bowl, and serve with chips or sliced veggies.

DEVILED POTATOES

DAIRY-FREE, GLUTEN-FREE, NUT-FREE

SERVES 6

PREP AND FINISHING: 25 MINUTES

PRESSURE COOK:
10 MINUTES ON HIGH

RELEASE: QUICK

TOTAL TIME: 45 MINUTES

USE IT UP: MAKE MASHED POTATOES WITH THE SCOOPED OUT PORTIONS OF THE POTATOES. ADD SOME CREAM OR MILK, SALT, PEPPER, AND CHIVES FOR A QUICK SIDE DISH.

Per Serving
Calories: 143; Fat: 4g;
Carbohydrates: 25g;
Fiber: 3g; Protein: 3g;
Sodium: 319mg

I love deviled eggs and wondered if it was possible to make something similar with a vegetable. I came up with a unique spin on a classic dish by turning to another staple in American cooking—potatoes! The potatoes make the ideal vessel and finger food. This crowd-pleaser is perfect for parties and potlucks—and budget-friendly to boot.

6 medium Yukon Gold potatoes (about 1½ pounds), halved

1 cup water

5 tablespoons mayonnaise

1 teaspoon Dijon mustard

1 tablespoon sweet pickle relish

1 teaspoon sugar

½ teaspoon freshly squeezed lemon juice

½ teaspoon kosher salt

½ teaspoon freshly ground black pepper

1 tablespoon finely chopped fresh cilantro

1 teaspoon paprika

1. **Pressure cook the potatoes.** Place the halved potatoes in the steamer rack. Pour the water into the inner pot, and place the trivet inside. Place the steamer rack on the trivet. Lock the lid into place. Select Pressure Cook or Manual, and adjust the pressure to High and the time to 10 minutes. Make sure the steam release knob is in the sealed position. After cooking, quick release the pressure. Unlock and remove the lid. Using tongs, carefully transfer the potatoes to a platter. Set aside to cool for 15 minutes.

2. **Prepare the filling.** In a medium bowl, mix together the mayonnaise, mustard, relish, sugar, lemon juice, salt and pepper.

3. **Assemble the Deviled Potatoes.** Using a melon scooper or spoon, remove the middle part of the potatoes, creating a well. Spoon 1 to 1½ teaspoons of filling into each potato. Garnish each deviled potato with the cilantro and paprika before serving.

CREAMY BEET AND CORN SALAD

DAIRY-FREE, GLUTEN-FREE, NUT-FREE

SERVES 6

PREP AND FINISHING:
30 MINUTES, PLUS
1 HOUR TO CHILL

PRESSURE COOK:
4 + 4 MINUTES ON HIGH

RELEASE: QUICK

TOTAL TIME: 1 HOUR 50 MINUTES

MAKE IT VEGAN: USE
VEGAN MAYO OR SKIP
THE MAYO ALTOGETHER
AND ADD 1/2 TABLESPOON
MORE OF OLIVE OIL.

Per Serving
Calories: 98; Fat: 5g;
Carbohydrates: 13g;
Fiber: 2g; Protein: 2g;
Sodium: 399mg

Add some color to your plate with this crunchy salad. It's perfect for make-ahead meals, as it stores really well in the refrigerator. You can also use it as a filling for wraps or in grain bowls. The beets and corn are also excellent sources of Vitamin C and fiber.

2 medium red beets, peeled (about 1 pound)

1 corn on the cob, husks removed, washed

1½ cups water

¼ cup finely chopped onion

¼ cup finely chopped fresh cilantro

3 tablespoons mayonnaise

1 tablespoon extra-virgin olive oil

2 teaspoons freshly squeezed lemon juice

1 teaspoon grated lemon zest

1 teaspoon sugar

1 teaspoon kosher salt

1 teaspoon freshly ground black pepper

1. **Pressure cook the beets and corn.** Place the whole beets and corn in the steamer rack. Pour the water into the inner pot, and place the trivet inside. Place the steamer rack on the trivet. Lock the lid into pace. Select Pressure Cook or Manual, and adjust the pressure to High and the time to 4 minutes. Make sure the steam release knob is in the sealed position. After cooking, quick release the pressure. Unlock and remove the lid. Using tongs, transfer the corn to a plate and set aside to cool. Lock the lid into place again and make sure the steam release valve is in the sealed position. Select Pressure Cook or Manual, and set the pressure to High and the time to 4 minutes. After cooking the beets, quick release the pressure. Unlock and remove the lid. Using tongs, transfer the beets to the plate with the corn and set aside to cool.

2. **Assemble the salad.** Using a knife, carefully remove the corn kernels from the cob. Cut the beets into ½-inch cubes. In a large bowl, combine the beets, corn, onion, cilantro, mayonnaise, olive oil, lemon juice and zest, sugar, salt, and pepper. Mix thoroughly and chill in the refrigerator for 1 hour. Serve.

GREEN BEAN STIR-FRY

DAIRY-FREE, VEGAN

SERVES 4

PREP AND FINISHING
20 MINUTES

STEAM: 1 MINUTE

SAUTÉ: 3 MINUTES

RELEASE: QUICK

TOTAL TIME: 35 MINUTES

TRY THIS: INSTEAD OF GREEN
BEANS, USE BRUSSELS SPROUTS,
BROCCOLI, OR ASPARAGUS—
ANY STURDY VEGETABLE
WORKS HERE. COOK TIME AND
PRESSURE REMAIN THE SAME
FOR THESE VEGETABLES.

Per Serving
Calories: 136; Fat: 6g;
Carbohydrates: 9g;
Fiber: 4g; Protein: 4g;
Sodium: 628mg

Since getting an Instant Pot®, green beans have become my favorite vegetable. They hold up well against pressure cooking without losing their color and texture. This sweet, spicy, garlicky recipe is now a family favorite.

12 ounces green
beans, trimmed

1 cup water

2 tablespoons corn oil

2 garlic cloves, finely chopped

3 tablespoons crushed peanuts

2 tablespoons soy sauce

¼ teaspoon kosher salt

½ teaspoon cane sugar

2 teaspoons chili flakes

1. **Pressure cook the beans.** Place the beans in the steamer basket. Pour the water into the inner pot, and place the trivet inside. Place the basket on the trivet. Lock the lid into place. Select Steam, and set the time to 1 minute. (For firmer beans, set the time to 0 minutes.) After cooking, quick release the pressure. Unlock and remove the lid. Drain the beans, and wipe the inner pot dry.

2. **Sauté the garlic and peanuts.** Select Sauté, and pour in the oil. Once hot, add the garlic and sauté for 1 minute. Add the peanuts and soy sauce, and sauté for 2 more minutes.

3. **Assemble the dish.** In a large bowl, combine the green beans, garlic, peanuts, salt, and sugar. Mix until the sugar and salt are dissolved. Sprinkle in some chili flakes, and serve hot.

BRUSSELS SPROUTS WITH BALSAMIC VINEGAR

DAIRY-FREE, GLUTEN-FREE, NUT-FREE, VEGAN

SERVES 4

PREP AND FINISHING: 15 MINUTES

STEAM: 1 MINUTE

RELEASE: QUICK

SAUTÉ: 3 MINUTES

TOTAL TIME: 30 MINUTES

TRY THIS: INSTEAD OF BRUSSELS SPROUTS, USE ASPARAGUS, BROCCOLI, OR GREEN BEANS. OR, TO SAVE TIME, JUST LEAVE THE BRUSSEL SPROUTS WHOLE AND ADD AN EXTRA MINUTE TO THE PRESSURE COOKING TIME.

Per Serving
Calories: 98; Fat: 5g; Carbohydrates: 12g; Fiber: 5g; Protein: 5g; Sodium: 612mg

Get your daily dose of valuable nutrients with these delicious Brussel sprouts. The balsamic vinegar and sesame seeds add balance and texture to the vegetables—a hint of sweet and tangy flavor, plus that extra crunch. It's a perfect side dish for any meal.

25 Brussels sprouts, halved lengthwise (about ¾ pound)

1 cup water

1 tablespoon extra-virgin olive oil

2 garlic cloves, finely chopped

1 tablespoon balsamic vinegar

1 teaspoon kosher salt

½ teaspoon freshly ground black pepper

1 tablespoon roasted sesame seeds

1. **Pressure cook the Brussels sprouts.** Place the Brussels sprouts in the steamer basket. Pour the water into the inner pot, and place the trivet inside. Place the basket on the trivet. Lock the lid into place. Select Steam, and set the time to 1 minute. Make sure the steam release knob is in the sealed position. After cooking, quick release the pressure. Unlock and remove the lid. Using tongs, carefully transfer the Brussels sprouts to a serving plate. Discard the water, and wipe the inner pot dry.

2. **Make the sauce.** Select Sauté, and pour in the oil. Once hot, add the garlic and sauté for 1 minute. Add the Brussels sprouts, vinegar, salt, and pepper, and sauté for 2 minutes. Sprinkle with the roasted sesame seeds and serve hot.

SZECHUAN HONEY-GLAZED ASPARAGUS

DAIRY-FREE, GLUTEN-FREE, NUT-FREE

SERVES 4

PREP AND FINISHING: 15 MINUTES

PRESSURE COOK:
1 MINUTE ON HIGH

RELEASE: QUICK

TOTAL TIME: 25 MINUTES

TRY THIS: TRY THIS RECIPE WITH BRUSSELS SPROUTS, BROCCOLI, OR GREEN BEANS. COOK TIME AND PRESSURE REMAIN THE SAME. IT'S ALSO WONDERFUL WITH A SWEET CHILI SAUCE. MIX TOGETHER 2 TABLESPOONS OF SWEET CHILI SAUCE WITH 1 TEASPOON OF SUGAR, AND DRIZZLE OVER THE ASPARAGUS OR OTHER VEGETABLES.

Per Serving
Calories: 88; Fat: 4g;
Carbohydrates: 14g;
Fiber: 2g; Protein: 2g;
Sodium: 418mg

Asparagus is a wonderfully versatile vegetable that brings elegance to any meal. Whether steamed or roasted, it's always delicious. With so few ingredients and so little cook time, you, too, can prepare this delicious asparagus dish that will be the hit of any meal.

2 bunches asparagus (about 24), woody ends removed

1 tablespoon extra-virgin olive oil

½ teaspoon kosher salt

½ teaspoon freshly ground black pepper

1 cup water

2 tablespoons honey

1 tablespoon Szechuan sauce

1. **Prepare the asparagus.** Place the asparagus in a large bowl. Drizzle with the olive oil, salt, and pepper, and toss to combine. Place the asparagus in the steaming rack.

2. **Pressure cook the asparagus.** Pour the water into the inner pot, and place the trivet inside. Place the steamer rack on the trivet. Lock the lid into place. Select Pressure Cook or Manual, and adjust the pressure to High and the time to 1 minute. (For firm and crunchy asparagus, set the time to 0 minutes.) After cooking, quick release the pressure.

3. **Assemble the asparagus.** Unlock and remove the lid. Using tongs, transfer the asparagus to a serving bowl. In a small bowl, combine the honey and Szechuan sauce. Drizzle over the asparagus, and serve hot.

SWEET POTATO GRATIN

NUT-FREE

....

SERVES 8

PREP AND FINISHING:
20 MINUTES, PLUS
1 HOUR TO COOL

PRESSURE COOK:
30 MINUTES ON HIGH

RELEASE: NATURAL

TOTAL TIME: 2 HOURS

....

TRY THIS: USE YUKON GOLD
POTATOES FOR A CLASSIC POTATO
AU GRATIN. THE PRESSURE
AND COOK TIMES REMAIN THE
SAME. TRADITIONAL BREAD
CRUMBS WORK WELL, TOO,
IF YOU DON'T HAVE PANKO
BREAD CRUMBS ON HAND.

....

Per Serving
Calories: 201; Fat: 15g;
Carbohydrates: 14g;
Fiber: 2g; Protein: 5g;
Sodium: 445mg

A traditional potato gratin is full of creamy goodness that can take a long time to prep and just as long to cook in the oven. No wonder it was saved for holidays or special occasions. My Instant Pot® take is made with sweet potatoes and topped with panko bread crumbs. It's so tasty and easy to prep, I guarantee you'll be making it year round.

2 medium sweet potatoes, peeled and thinly sliced (about 1 pound)

2 tablespoons extra-virgin olive oil

1 teaspoon kosher salt

1 teaspoon freshly ground black pepper

1 tablespoon dried basil

1 tablespoon dried thyme

1 tablespoon butter, melted

½ cup heavy (whipping) cream

1 cup Mexican-blend shredded cheese

2 tablespoons panko bread crumbs

1 cup water

1. Prepare the sweet potatoes. In a large bowl, drizzle the olive oil over the sweet potato slices. Season with the salt, pepper, basil, and thyme. Mix thoroughly to coat the sweet potatoes. Set aside. In a small bowl, mix together the butter and cream.

2. Assemble the gratin. In a springform pan, arrange a single layer of sweet potatoes. Spread about 2 tablespoons of the cream-butter mixture on top, and sprinkle with 4 to 5 tablespoons of the cheese. Repeat these steps until all of the sweet potato slices have been used, about three layers. After the last layer, sprinkle the bread crumbs on top. Cover the pan with aluminum foil.

3. Pressure cook the gratin. Pour the water into the inner pot, and place the trivet inside. Place the springform pan on the trivet. Lock the lid into place. Select Pressure Cook or Manual, and adjust the pressure to High and the time to 30 minutes. Make sure the steam release knob is in the sealed position. After cooking, naturally release the pressure. Unlock and remove the lid. Carefully remove the pan. Let the sweet potatoes cool for at least 1 hour before serving so the cheese sets.

SPAGHETTI SQUASH WITH PESTO

GLUTEN-FREE

SERVES 6

PREP AND FINISHING: 25 MINUTES

PRESSURE COOK:
12 MINUTES ON HIGH

RELEASE: NATURAL
10 MINUTES, THEN QUICK

TOTAL TIME: 1 HOUR

MAKE IT DAIRY-FREE, NUT-FREE, AND VEGAN: INSTEAD OF PESTO, MIX IN EXTRA-VIRGIN OLIVE OIL, CHERRY TOMATOES, AND FRESH BASIL TO MAKE A LIGHT PASTA SALAD.

Per Serving
Calories: 115; Fat: 6g;
Carbohydrates: 13g;
Fiber: 0g; Protein: 3g;
Sodium: 102mg

For all you low-carb lovers, here is a perfect veggie "noodle" that doesn't require a spiralizer. I usually mix my own home-made pesto into the squash noodles, but you can use other sauces—store bought or homemade—to make it your own.

1½ cups plus 3 tablespoons water, divided

1 (roughly 3-pound) spaghetti squash, pierced with a knife about 10 times

¼ cup pesto

1. Pressure cook the spaghetti squash. Pour 1½ cups of water into the inner pot, and place the trivet inside. Place the squash on the trivet. Lock the lid into place. Select Pressure Cook or Manual, and adjust the pressure to High and the time to 12 minutes. Make sure the steam release knob is in the sealed position. After cooking, release the pressure naturally for 10 minutes, then quick release any remaining pressure. Unlock and remove the lid. Using tongs, carefully transfer the squash to a cutting board to cool for about 10 minutes.

2. Shred the squash. Halve the spaghetti squash length-wise. Using a spoon, scoop out and discard the seeds. Using a fork, scrape the flesh of the squash and shred into long "noodles." Place the noodles in a medium serving bowl.

3. Assemble the spaghetti squash. In a small bowl, mix the pesto with the remaining 3 tablespoons of water. Drizzle over the squash, toss to combine, and serve warm.

ETHIOPIAN-STYLE VEGETABLE CURRY

DAIRY-FREE, GLUTEN-FREE, NUT-FREE, VEGAN

SERVES 6

PREP AND FINISHING: 20 MINUTES

STEAM: 5 MINUTES

RELEASE: QUICK

SAUTÉ: 7 MINUTES

TOTAL TIME: 40 MINUTES

PAIR IT: SERVE THIS DISH ALONGSIDE *INJERA*, A TRADITIONAL AFRICAN FLATBREAD, FOR A COMPLETE MEAL.

TRY THIS: USE BUTTERNUT SQUASH, SWEET POTATOES, OR PURPLE CABBAGE FOR THIS DISH. FOR THE BUTTERNUT SQUASH, INCREASE THE COOK TIME TO 6 TO 7 MINUTES, AND FOR THE SWEET POTATO, INCREASE COOK TIME TO 8 MINUTES. PRESSURE REMAINS THE SAME.

Per Serving
Calories: 65; Fat: 2g;
Carbohydrates: 12g;
Fiber: 3g; Protein: 2g;
Sodium: 508mg

In Ethiopian cuisine, spicy vegetable curries, known as Tikel Gomen Mitmita, are a home-cooking standard. They usually call for traditional Ethiopian spices—a combination of bird's eye chiles, cardamom seeds, cloves, and salt. My take uses curry powder, which you can find in the spice section of your local grocery store.

2 medium carrots, cut into 1-inch pieces

3 cups roughly shredded green cabbage

2 Yukon Gold potatoes, cut into 1-inch pieces (about ½ pound)

1 cup water

2 teaspoons corn oil

½ onion, finely chopped

1 garlic clove, finely chopped

1 teaspoon freshly grated ginger

1 tablespoon mild curry powder

1¼ teaspoons kosher salt

1 tablespoon finely chopped fresh cilantro, for garnish

1. Steam the vegetables. Place the carrots, cabbage, and potatoes in the steamer rack. Add the water to the inner pot, and place the trivet inside. Place the steamer rack on the trivet. Lock the lid into place. Select Steam, and set the time to 5 minutes. Make sure the steam release knob is in the sealed position. After cooking, quick release the pressure. Unlock and remove the lid. Place the vegetables in a colander. Discard the water.

2. Prepare the curry. Wipe the inside of the pot dry, and return it to its place. Select Sauté, and pour in the oil. Once hot, add the onion, garlic, and ginger, and sauté until the onion turns translucent, about 3 minutes. Add the curry powder and salt, and sauté for 2 minutes. Add the steamed vegetables and cook, stirring frequently, for about 2 minutes. Transfer the curry to a serving platter, garnish with the cilantro, and serve hot.

KUNG PAO BROCCOLI WITH TOFU

DAIRY-FREE, VEGAN

SERVES 4

PREP AND FINISHING: 20 MINUTES

SAUTÉ: 3 MINUTES

PRESSURE COOK:
1 MINUTE ON HIGH

RELEASE: QUICK

TOTAL TIME: 35 MINUTES

PAIR IT: SERVE THIS DISH ALONG WITH RICE, UDON NOODLES, OR LO MEIN FOR A COMPLETE MEAL.

Per Serving
Calories: 180; Fat: 12g;
Carbohydrates: 15g;
Fiber: 4g; Protein: 6g;
Sodium: 575mg

Traditional Chinese kung pao is usually served with chicken. My vegetarian take uses tofu instead. Most importantly, it has the same traditional flavor as the kung pao you likely enjoy from your favorite takeout place. I like to serve my version with jasmine rice.

1¼ cups water

1 tablespoon cornstarch

1 tablespoon rice vinegar

1 tablespoon soy sauce

1 tablespoon Sriracha

1 teaspoon sugar

½ teaspoon kosher salt

2 tablespoons peanut oil

10 scallions, chopped, white and green parts separated

1 garlic clove, finely chopped

3 dried Thai red chiles

1 teaspoon freshly ground black pepper

3 whole cloves

2 cups broccoli florets, cut into bite-size pieces (about 10 ounces)

¾ cup bite-size pieces red and green bell pepper mix

½ cup (1-inch cubes) extra-firm tofu, pressed to remove water

¼ cup peanuts

1. Prepare the slurry. In a small mixing bowl, stir together the water and cornstarch. Mix thoroughly and set aside.

2. Prepare the sauce. In a medium bowl, mix together the vinegar, soy sauce, Sriracha, sugar, and salt. Set aside.

3. Sauté the vegetables. Select Sauté, and pour in the oil. Once hot, add the white parts of the scallions and the garlic, chiles, black pepper, and cloves. Sauté for 2 minutes. Add the broccoli, bell pepper, tofu, peanuts, and sauce. Mix thoroughly. Add the slurry, and stir constantly until everything is well combined.

4. Pressure cook the kung pao. Lock the lid into place. Select Pressure Cook or Manual, and adjust the pressure to High and the time to 1 minute. After cooking, quick release the pressure. Unlock and remove the lid. Stir the kung pao once before transferring to a serving bowl. *Do not keep the kung pao in Keep Warm mode, as the broccoli might become soft and mushy.* Garnish with the green parts of the scallions, and serve hot.

BRAZILIAN-STYLE VEGETABLE CURRY

DAIRY-FREE, GLUTEN-
FREE, NUT-FREE, VEGAN

SERVES 8

PREP AND FINISHING: 20 MINUTES

SAUTÉ: 5 MINUTES

PRESSURE COOK: 5 +
3 MINUTES ON HIGH

RELEASE: QUICK

TOTAL TIME: 45 MINUTES

MAKE IT A MEAL: SERVE THIS
CURRY WITH CILANTRO-LIME
RICE (PAGE 79), LEMONY NAVY
BEAN SALAD (PAGE 40), AND
SWEET CORN TAMALITO (PAGE
104) FOR A FOUR-COURSE MEAL.

Per Serving
Calories: 154; Fat: 10g;
Carbohydrates: 14g;
Fiber: 4g; Protein: 3g;
Sodium: 391mg

Coconut milk is a signature staple of South American cuisines. It's the secret ingredient that makes so many dishes in Brazilian cooking delicious and decadent, especially curry. In this recipe, the butternut squash and eggplant have different cooking times, so make sure to add the butternut squash first, then the eggplant.

3 Roma tomatoes, chopped

½ cup roughly chopped yellow onion

1 Thai green chile, chopped

1 dried red chile

2 garlic cloves, finely chopped

1 teaspoon finely chopped fresh ginger

½ cup water

2 teaspoons corn oil

2 cups (1-inch cubes) butternut squash

1 (14-ounce) can full-fat coconut milk

1¼ teaspoons kosher salt

1 medium eggplant, cut into bite-size pieces

1 cup chopped red, orange, or yellow bell pepper or a mix

2 tablespoons chopped fresh cilantro

1. **Prepare the tomato paste.** In a blender, roughly grind the tomatoes, onion, green chile, red chile, garlic, and ginger with the water.

2. **Sauté the tomato paste.** Select Sauté, and pour the oil into the inner pot. Once hot, slowly pour in the tomato paste mixture. Sauté for about 5 minutes, until the onions are translucent. Add the butternut squash, coconut milk, and salt.

3. Pressure cook the butternut squash. Lock the lid into place. Select Pressure Cook or Manual, and adjust the pressure to High and the time to 5 minutes. Make sure the steam release knob in in the sealed position. After cooking, quick release the pressure.

4. Pressure cook the eggplant. Unlock and remove the lid. Scrape the bottom of the pot with a wooden spoon, ensuring nothing is sticking to the bottom. Add the eggplant and bell pepper. Lock the lid into place. Select Manual, and adjust the pressure to High and the time to 3 minutes. After cooking, quick release the pressure. Unlock and remove the lid. Stir the curry, and garnish with the cilantro. Serve hot.

THAI-STYLE VEGETABLE CURRY

DAIRY-FREE, GLUTEN-
FREE, NUT-FREE, VEGAN

SERVES 6

PREP AND FINISHING: 20 MINUTES

SAUTÉ: 3 MINUTES

PRESSURE COOK:
2 MINUTES ON HIGH

RELEASE: NATURAL
5 MINUTES, THEN QUICK

TOTAL TIME: 40 MINUTES

MAKE IT NEW: THE THAI CURRY
PASTE ALSO MAKES EXCELLENT
THAI CURRY RICE. AFTER
SAUTÉING THE VEGETABLES,
ADD 1¹/₂ CUPS OF RICE AND
3 CUPS OF WATER. PRESSURE
COOK FOR 6 MINUTES ON HIGH.
AFTER COOKING, NATURALLY
RELEASE THE PRESSURE FOR
3 MINUTES, THEN QUICK RELEASE
THE REMAINING PRESSURE.

Per Serving
Calories: 182; Fat: 15g;
Carbohydrates: 11g;
Fiber: 3g; Protein: 3g;
Sodium: 406mg

I love Thai Cuisine. But, being a vegetarian, I don't use store-bought Thai curry pastes, since they usually contain fish sauce. I finally decided to make my own, which I've included here. It's as delicious as any you find in a restaurant—even my 9-year-old approves. For convenience, you can use store-bought curry paste instead.

FOR THE THAI CURRY PASTE

3 dried red Thai chiles

½ teaspoon cumin seeds

1 teaspoon coriander seeds

½ teaspoon whole black peppercorns

2 garlic cloves

1 tablespoon finely chopped fresh cilantro

¼ cup chopped onion

1 tablespoon finely chopped fresh ginger

1 tablespoon sliced lemongrass

3 tablespoons water

FOR THE VEGETABLE CURRY

2 teaspoons corn oil

½ cup (1-inch pieces) chopped carrots

½ cup (1-inch cubed) peeled potatoes

5 fresh snap peas

5 fresh baby corn ears, cut into bite-size pieces

1 teaspoon kosher salt

1 teaspoon sugar

¼ teaspoon ground turmeric

1 (12-ounce) can full-fat coconut milk

½ cup (½-inch cubes) extra-firm tofu, pressed to remove water

6 fresh basil leaves, roughly chopped

1. **Prepare the Thai curry paste.** In a blender, blend the chiles, cumin seeds, coriander seeds, peppercorns, garlic, cilantro, onion, ginger, lemongrass, and water into a smooth paste.

2. **Sauté the vegetables.** Select Sauté, and pour in the oil. Once hot, add the carrots, potatoes, snap peas, baby corn, salt, sugar, and turmeric, and sauté for 1 minute. Add the curry paste, and sauté for 2 more minutes. Add the coconut milk, tofu, and half of the basil, and mix thoroughly.

3. **Pressure cook the vegetable curry.** Lock the lid into place. Select Pressure Cook or Manual, and adjust the pressure to High and the time to 2 minutes. After cooking, naturally release the pressure for 5 minutes, then quick release any remaining pressure. Unlock and remove the lid. Serve, garnished with the remaining basil.

MIXED-VEGETABLE KORMA

SERVES 6

PREP AND FINISHING: 20 MINUTES

PRESSURE COOK:
2 + 3 MINUTES ON HIGH

SAUTÉ: 2 MINUTES

RELEASE: QUICK

TOTAL TIME: 35 MINUTES

INGREDIENT TIP: INSTEAD
OF CASHEWS, YOU CAN USE
BLANCHED ALMONDS OR
SHELLED PISTACHIOS. FOR A
RICHER GRAVY, YOU CAN USE A
COMBINATION OF ALL THREE
NUTS OR ANY TWO VARIETIES.

Per Serving
Calories: 133; Fat: 7g;
Carbohydrates: 14g; Fiber: 3g;
Protein: 4g; Sodium: 349mg

In India, Navratan Korma is a well-known mixed vegetable dish made with cream. *Navratan* means "nine gems." In this recipe, I've cut back on the long list of ingredients for you. All you need is some curry powder and allspice to get that perfect flavor. Serve with naan or basmati rice for a delicious meal.

½ cup chopped onion

10 raw cashews

1 green Thai chile, finely chopped

1 cup water, divided

1 large carrot, chopped into 1-inch cubes (about ¾ cup)

1 medium potato, peeled and cut into 1-inch cubes (about ½ cup)

1¼ cups cauliflower florets (about ½ pound)

¼ cup frozen peas

1 teaspoon curry powder

½ teaspoon ground allspice

1 teaspoon kosher salt

⅓ cup heavy (whipping) cream

2 tablespoons finely chopped fresh cilantro

1 tablespoon roughly chopped fresh mint leaves

Naan bread or Turmeric Rice (page 78), for serving

1. **Pressure cook the onion-cashew paste.** Add the onion, cashews, green chile, and ½ cup of water to the inner pot. Lock the lid into place. Select Pressure Cook or Manual, and adjust the pressure to High and the time to 2 minutes. Make sure the steam release knob is in the sealed position. After cooking, quick release the pressure. Unlock and remove the lid. Use an immersion blender to purée the mixture.

2. **Pressure cook the korma.** Select Sauté. Once hot, add the carrot, potato, cauliflower, peas, curry powder, allspice, salt, cream, and remaining ½ cup of water to the onion-cashew paste. Mix thoroughly, and sauté for 2 minutes. Lock the lid into place. Select Pressure Cook or Manual, and adjust the pressure to High and the time to 3 minutes. Make sure the steam release knob is in the sealed position. After cooking, quick release the pressure. Unlock and remove the lid. Add the chopped cilantro and mint leaves, and stir the korma one last time. Serve hot with naan bread or Turmeric Rice (see page 78).

Chickpea Greek Salad

PAGE 37

Chapter Three
BEANS AND LEGUMES

HUMMUS

DAIRY-FREE, GLUTEN-
FREE, NUT-FREE, VEGAN

SERVES 6

PREP AND FINISHING: 5 MINUTES,
PLUS AT LEAST 6 HOURS TO SOAK

PRESSURE COOK:
20 MINUTES ON HIGH

RELEASE: NATURAL

TOTAL TIME: 6 HOURS 35 MINUTES

MAKE IT NEW: SPREAD THE
HUMMUS IN A PITA AND FILL
WITH CHICKPEA GREEK SALAD
(PAGE 37) AND SOME GREENS
FOR A FILLING SANDWICH.

Per Serving
Calories: 52; Fat: 5g;
Carbohydrates: 2g;
Fiber: 1g; Protein: 1g;
Sodium: 217mg

Hummus is a must-have, protein-rich vegetarian dish, and this simple recipe is one of my favorites. I use it as a spread in my sandwiches and wraps, or as a dip with pita chips or fresh vegetables. In addition to protein and fiber, chickpeas are an excellent source of vitamin K and folate, so go ahead and indulge.

½ cup dried chickpeas

1½ cups water

1 teaspoon hot chili sauce

½ teaspoon kosher salt

2 garlic cloves,
roughly chopped

2 tablespoons extra-virgin
olive oil

1 tablespoon freshly squeezed
lemon juice

½ teaspoon paprika,
for garnish

1. Soak the beans. In a large bowl, cover the chickpeas with 2 to 3 inches of cold water. Soak at room temperature for 6 to 8 hours, or overnight. Drain and rinse.

2. Pressure cook the beans. Pour the water into the inner pot, and add the chickpeas. Lock the lid into place. Select Pressure Cook or Manual, and adjust the pressure to High and the time to 20 minutes. Make sure the steam release knob is in the sealed position. After cooking, naturally release the pressure. Unlock and remove the lid. Drain the beans and let cool for about 5 minutes.

3. Prepare the hummus. In a blender, combine the beans, chili sauce, salt, garlic, olive oil, and lemon juice, and blend until smooth. Transfer to a serving dish, sprinkle with the paprika, and serve.

CHICKPEA GREEK SALAD

GLUTEN-FREE, NUT-FREE

SERVES 6

PREP AND FINISHING: 10 MINUTES,
PLUS AT LEAST 6 HOURS TO SOAK

PRESSURE COOK:
15 MINUTES ON HIGH

RELEASE: NATURAL

TOTAL TIME: 6 HOURS 35 MINUTES

TRY THIS: YOU CAN MAKE THIS
SALAD WITH KIDNEY BEANS OR
NAVY BEANS. YOU WON'T NEED
TO ADJUST THE PRESSURE OR
COOK TIME FOR EITHER SWAP.

MAKE IT VEGAN: SKIP THE FETA
CHEESE TO MAKE IT VEGAN.

Per Serving
Calories: 98; Fat: 7g;
Carbohydrates: 8g;
Fiber: 2g; Protein: 3g;
Sodium: 434mg

Healthy, light, and refreshing, this Mediterranean-style chickpea salad is tossed with red wine vinegar dressing. It's perfect for spring and summer picnics, but I also make it year round. Cook a large batch of chickpeas over the weekend, and make this your go-to weekday meal.

1 cup dried chickpeas	10 cherry tomatoes, halved
3 cups water	10 pitted black olives, halved
2 tablespoons extra-virgin olive oil	1 cucumber, cut into ½-inch dice
1 tablespoon red wine vinegar	¼ cup chopped green bell pepper
1 teaspoon kosher salt	2 tablespoons finely chopped fresh cilantro
½ teaspoon freshly ground black pepper	1 ounce feta cheese, crumbled
½ cup finely chopped onion	

1. Soak the beans. In a large bowl, cover the chickpeas with 2 to 3 inches of cold water. Soak at room temperature for 6 to 8 hours, or overnight. Drain and rinse.

2. Pressure cook the beans. Pour the water into the inner pot and add the chickpeas. Lock the lid into place. Select Pressure Cook or Manual, and adjust the pressure to High and the time to 15 minutes. Make sure the steam release knob is in the sealed position. After cooking, naturally release the pressure. Unlock and remove the lid. Drain the beans and let cool for about 5 minutes.

3. Prepare the dressing. In a small jar or bowl, combine the olive oil, vinegar, salt, and black pepper. Seal and shake or whisk thoroughly.

4. Assemble the salad. In a large bowl, combine the chickpeas, onion, cherry tomatoes, olives, cucumber, bell pepper, and cilantro. Add the dressing and toss. Top with the feta and serve cold.

QUINOA AND BLACK BEAN SALAD

DAIRY-FREE, GLUTEN-FREE, NUT-FREE, VEGAN

SERVES 8

PREP AND FINISHING: 15 MINUTES, PLUS AT LEAST 6 HOURS TO SOAK

PRESSURE COOK:
8 MINUTES ON HIGH

RELEASE: NATURAL

TOTAL TIME: 6 HOURS 35 MINUTES

TRY THIS: INSTEAD OF BLACK BEANS, YOU CAN USE KIDNEY BEANS OR PINTO BEANS FOR THIS SALAD. PRESSURE COOK THE KIDNEY BEANS FOR 25 MINUTES AND THE PINTO BEANS FOR 20 TO 25 MINUTES. PRESSURE AND STEAM RELEASE METHODS REMAIN THE SAME.

Per Serving
Calories: 218; Fat: 7g;
Carbohydrates: 32g;
Fiber: 6g; Protein: 9g;
Sodium: 338mg

This quinoa salad is the perfect choice for a midday meal. The quinoa and black beans combine nicely with the corn and bell pepper. Plus, this bean and grain combination delivers a complete protein, which will keep you satisfied for a long time.

1 cup dried black beans

1 cup quinoa, rinsed and drained

5 cups water, divided

1 tablespoon red wine vinegar

3 tablespoons extra-virgin olive oil

1 teaspoon ground cumin

2 teaspoons freshly ground black pepper

2 tablespoons freshly squeezed lemon juice

1½ teaspoons kosher salt

1 green bell pepper, cut into ½-inch dice

2 serrano chiles, finely chopped

¼ cup frozen corn kernels, thawed to room temperature

¼ cup finely chopped fresh cilantro

2 shallots, finely chopped

1. **Soak the beans.** In a large bowl, cover the black beans with 2 to 3 inches of cold water. Soak at room temperature for 6 to 8 hours, or overnight. Drain and rinse.

2. **Pressure cook the beans and the quinoa.** Put the quinoa in a stackable pan, and add 1½ cups of water. In another stackable pan, put the beans and 2 cups of water. Place the pan with the quinoa on top of the pan with the beans. Close the pan lids and place them on the interlocking handle. Pour the remaining 1½ cups of water in the inner pot, and place the trivet inside. Place the stackable pans on the trivet. Lock the lid into place. Select Pressure Cook or Manual, and adjust the pressure to High and the time to 8 minutes. Make sure the steam release knob is in the sealed position. After cooking, naturally release the pressure. Unlock and remove the lid. Drain the beans, and fluff the quinoa with a fork. Set both aside to cool for 5 minutes.

3. **Prepare the dressing.** In a small jar or bowl, combine the vinegar, olive oil, cumin, black pepper, lemon juice, and salt. Seal and shake or whisk thoroughly.

4. **Assemble the salad.** In a large bowl, combine the quinoa, black beans, bell pepper, chiles, corn, cilantro, and shallots. Pour the dressing over the salad, toss to combine, and serve.

LEMONY NAVY BEAN SALAD

DAIRY-FREE, GLUTEN-FREE, NUT-FREE, VEGAN

SERVES 6

PREP AND FINISHING:
5 MINUTES, PLUS 6 HOURS TO
SOAK AND 1 HOUR TO CHILL

PRESSURE COOK:
15 MINUTES ON HIGH

RELEASE: NATURAL

TOTAL TIME: 7 HOURS 30 MINUTES

PAIR IT: SERVE THIS SALAD ALONG
WITH THE SPICY JOLLOF RICE
(PAGE 80) FOR A COMPLETE MEAL.

Per Serving
Calories: 151; Fat: 3g;
Carbohydrates: 25g;
Fiber: 6g; Protein: 9g;
Sodium: 300mg

Navy beans are traditionally used in soups, but I like to use them in salads, too. It's an unexpected choice—and a great way to mix things up. The beans readily absorb the lemony dressing, and they hold up really well to pressure cooking.

1 cup dried navy beans

2 cups water

1 tablespoon extra-virgin olive oil

2 tablespoons freshly squeezed lemon juice

2 tablespoons grated lemon zest

1 teaspoon kosher salt

1 teaspoon freshly ground black pepper

½ cup finely chopped onion

1 cucumber, cut into ½-inch cubes

½ cup grated carrot

2 tablespoons finely chopped fresh parsley

1. **Soak the beans.** In a large bowl, cover the navy beans with 2 to 3 inches of cold water. Soak at room temperature for 6 hours. Drain and rinse.

2. **Pressure cook the beans.** Pour the water into the inner pot, and add the beans. Lock the lid into place. Select Pressure Cook or Manual, and adjust the pressure to High and the time to 15 minutes. Make sure the steam release knob is in the sealed position. After cooking, naturally release the pressure. Unlock and remove the lid. Drain the beans and let cool for 5 minutes.

3. **Prepare the dressing.** In a small jar or bowl, combine the olive oil, lemon juice and zest, salt, and pepper. Seal and shake, or whisk thoroughly.

4. **Assemble the salad.** In a medium bowl, combine the beans, onion, cucumber, carrot, and parsley. Add the dressing, and toss to combine. Refrigerate for 1 hour, and serve chilled.

CANNELLINI BEAN AND SPINACH SOUP

**DAIRY-FREE, GLUTEN-
FREE, NUT-FREE, VEGAN**

SERVES 8

PREP AND FINISHING: 15 MINUTES,
PLUS 4 HOURS TO SOAK

PRESSURE COOK:
8 + 10 MINUTES ON HIGH

RELEASE: NATURAL + NATURAL
5 MINUTES, THEN QUICK

SAUTÉ: 5 MINUTES

TOTAL TIME: 4 HOURS 55 MINUTES

MAKE IT A MEAL: SERVE THIS
SOUP ALONG WITH POLENTA
WITH MUSHROOMS (PAGE 103)
TO MAKE A COMPLETE MEAL.

Per Serving
Calories: 128; Fat: 4g;
Carbohydrates: 17g;
Fiber: 7g; Protein: 7g;
Sodium: 563mg

This soup of cannellini beans and spinach is a hearty and colorful bowl of warmth and it's all you need on a chilly day. And with the Instant Pot®, it can be ready in no time. Serve it with rustic bread for a hearty meal.

1 cup dried cannellini beans

3 cups water, divided

2 tablespoons corn oil

2 shallots, finely chopped

2 garlic cloves, finely chopped

1 medium carrot, grated

2 tomatoes, finely chopped

5 ounces fresh spinach leaves

2½ teaspoons kosher salt

1 teaspoon freshly ground black pepper

1 cup vegetable broth

2 tablespoons chopped fresh basil leaves, divided

1. Soak the beans. In a large bowl, cover the cannellini beans with 2 to 3 inches of cold water. Soak at room temperature for 4 hours. Drain and rinse.

2. Pressure cook the beans. Pour 2 cups of water into the inner pot, and add the beans. Lock the lid into place. Select Pressure Cook or Manual, and adjust the pressure to High and the time to 8 minutes. Make sure the steam release knob is in the sealed position. After cooking, naturally release the pressure. Unlock and remove the lid. Drain the beans, and set aside. Wipe out the inner pot.

3. Sauté the vegetables. Select Sauté, and pour in the oil. Once hot, add the shallots and garlic and sauté for 1 minute. Add the carrot, tomatoes, spinach, salt, and pepper. Cook until the spinach wilts, 4 to 5 minutes. Add the beans and broth, the remaining 1 cup of water, and 1 tablespoon of basil.

4. Pressure cook the soup. Lock the lid into place. Select Soup, and adjust the pressure to High and the time to 10 minutes. Make sure the steam release knob is in the sealed position. After cooking, naturally release the pressure for 5 minutes, then quick release any remaining pressure. Unlock and remove the lid. Stir in the remaining tablespoon of basil, and serve hot.

BLACK BEAN TORTILLA SOUP

**DAIRY-FREE, GLUTEN-
FREE, NUT-FREE, VEGAN**

SERVES 10

PREP AND FINISHING: 10 MINUTES,
PLUS AT LEAST 6 HOURS TO SOAK

SAUTÉ: 5 MINUTES

PRESSURE COOK:
30 MINUTES ON HIGH

RELEASE: NATURAL

TOTAL TIME: 7 HOURS

PAIR IT: SERVE THIS SOUP
ALONG WITH SPINACH OR
ANY GREEN LEAF SALAD TO
MAKE A COMPLETE MEAL.

Per Serving
Calories: 129; Fat: 3g;
Carbohydrates: 20g;
Fiber: 4g; Protein: 7g;
Sodium: 634mg

A sweet and spicy Black Bean Tortilla Soup—comfort food at its best. My version includes corn, which gives the soup extra flavor and texture. Top it with crunchy bits of corn tortilla chips, and I guarantee it will be hard to stop at just one bowl.

1 cup dried black beans

1 tablespoon corn oil

1 yellow onion, finely chopped

¼ cup finely chopped orange bell pepper

¼ cup frozen corn kernels, thawed to room temperature

½ teaspoon ground cumin

½ teaspoon dark chili powder

¼ teaspoon chipotle chili powder

2 teaspoons sugar

1 teaspoon kosher salt

1 (16-ounce) jar medium salsa

3 cups vegetable broth

1 cup water

¼ cup crumbled tortilla chips

1. **Soak the beans.** In a large bowl, cover the black beans with 2 to 3 inches of cold water. Soak at room temperature for 6 to 8 hours, or overnight. Drain and rinse.

2. **Sauté the vegetables.** Select Sauté, and pour in the oil. Once hot, add the onion and sauté until translucent, about 5 minutes. Add the bell pepper, corn, cumin, dark chili powder, chipotle chili powder, sugar, and salt. Press Cancel, and stir to combine. Stir in the salsa, broth, water, and beans.

3. **Pressure cook the beans.** Lock the lid into place. Select Bean/Chili, and adjust the pressure to High and the time to 30 minutes. Make sure the steam release knob is in the sealed position. After cooking, naturally release the pressure. Unlock and remove the lid. Stir the soup. Serve with the crumbled chips on top.

REFRIED BEANS

DAIRY-FREE, GLUTEN-FREE, NUT-FREE, VEGAN

SERVES 8

PREP AND FINISHING: 5 MINUTES, PLUS 3 HOURS TO SOAK

SAUTÉ: 7 MINUTES

PRESSURE COOK: 30 MINUTES ON HIGH

RELEASE: NATURAL

TOTAL TIME: 3 HOURS 50 MINUTES

MAKE IT NEW: FOR AN EASY AND DELICIOUS BEAN AND CHEESE QUESADILLA, SPREAD THE REFRIED BEANS OVER A FLOUR TORTILLA AND TOP IT WITH SHREDDED CHEDDAR OR MEXICAN-BLEND SHREDDED CHEESE. FOLD IN HALF AND PLACE IN A HOT SKILLET OVER MEDIUM HEAT. HEAT UNTIL GOLDEN BROWN, THEN FLIP AND CONTINUE COOKING UNTIL GOLDEN BROWN AND THE CHEESE IS MELTED.

Per Serving
Calories: 189; Fat: 3g;
Carbohydrates: 32g;
Fiber: 8g; Protein: 11g;
Sodium: 235mg

I love Mexican food, and refried beans are one of my favorites. But canned beans come with a high sodium content and, in some instances, additional preservatives. I prefer to make my own beans so I can cook them to my desired flavor and texture. My recipe always delivers perfectly creamy, rich beans; you won't ever bother with store-bought refried beans again.

2 cups dried pinto beans

1 tablespoon extra-virgin olive oil

½ yellow onion, finely chopped

3 garlic cloves, finely chopped

1 teaspoon ground cumin

1 teaspoon chili powder

½ teaspoon dried oregano

2 cups water

1 teaspoon kosher salt

1. Soak the beans. In a large bowl, cover the pinto beans with 2 to 3 inches of cold water. Soak at room temperature for 3 hours. Drain and rinse.

2. Sauté the onion and garlic. Select Sauté, and pour in the oil. Once hot, add the onion and garlic. Sauté until the onion is translucent, about 5 minutes. Add the beans, followed by the cumin, chili powder, and oregano, and stir for 2 minutes. Add the water and stir.

3. Pressure cook the beans. Lock the lid into place. Select Bean, and adjust the pressure to High and the time to 30 minutes. Make sure the steam release knob is in the sealed position. After cooking, naturally release the pressure. Unlock and remove the lid. Stir once, then stir in the salt.

4. Purée the beans. Using an immersion blender, purée the bean mixture until smooth and creamy. Serve hot.

BAKED BEANS

**DAIRY-FREE, GLUTEN-
FREE, NUT-FREE, VEGAN**

SERVES 10

PREP AND FINISHING: 10 MINUTES,
PLUS 4 HOURS TO SOAK

PRESSURE COOK: 15 +
15 MINUTES ON HIGH

RELEASE: NATURAL

SAUTÉ: 7 MINUTES

TOTAL TIME: 5 HOURS

MAKE IT NEW: FOR AN
INTERESTING TWIST, MIX THE
BAKED BEANS WITH BROCCOLI,
BRUSSELS SPROUTS, OR
ASPARAGUS. STEAM ANY ONE
OF THESE VEGETABLES ON HIGH
FOR 1 MINUTE, THEN QUICK
RELEASE THE PRESSURE.

Per Serving
Calories: 253; Fat: 2g;
Carbohydrates: 50g;
Fiber: 11g; Protein: 10g;
Sodium: 180mg

Traditional baked bean recipes call for some type of salted pork or bacon. My vegetarian spin swaps out the meat for red bell pepper to add depth and flavor, without the meat. Using your Instant Pot® to make these beans also cuts the cooking time in half, compared to the stove top method. I prefer to use vegan Worcestershire sauce in my recipe, but traditional Worcestershire sauce, which has anchovy as an ingredient, can also be used here.

12 ounces dried navy beans

2 cups water

1 tablespoon corn oil

1 yellow onion, finely chopped

½ cup finely chopped red
bell pepper

2 garlic cloves, finely chopped

½ cup molasses

¼ cup ketchup

1 tablespoon vegan
Worcestershire sauce

1 teaspoon kosher salt

3 tablespoons sugar

2 teaspoons hot sauce

1. Soak the beans. In a large bowl, cover the pinto beans with 2 to 3 inches of cold water. Soak at room temperature for 4 hours. Drain and rinse.

2. Pressure cook the beans. Pour the water into the inner pot, and add the beans. Lock the lid into place. Select Pressure Cook or Manual, and adjust the pressure to High and set the time to 15 minutes. Make sure the steam release knob is in the sealed position. After cooking, naturally release the pressure. Transfer the beans and water (do not drain) to a large bowl. Wipe the inner pot dry.

3. Make the sauce. Select Sauté, and pour in the oil. Once hot, add the onion and sauté until translucent, about 5 minutes. Add the bell pepper and garlic, and sauté for 2 minutes more. Stir in the molasses, ketchup, Worcestershire sauce, salt, sugar, and hot sauce. Stir in the beans and water.

4. Pressure cook the Baked Beans. Lock the lid into place. Select Pressure Cook or Manual, and adjust the pressure to High and the time to 15 minutes. Make sure the steam release knob is in the sealed position. After cooking, naturally release the pressure. Unlock and remove the lid. Serve hot.

YELLOW SPLIT PEAS WITH TURMERIC

DAIRY-FREE, GLUTEN-
FREE, NUT-FREE, VEGAN

SERVES 6

PREP AND FINISHING: 20 MINUTES

SAUTÉ: 6 MINUTES

PRESSURE COOK:
15 MINUTES ON HIGH

RELEASE: NATURAL

TOTAL TIME: 50 MINUTES

PAIR IT: PAIR THIS DISH WITH
SZECHUAN HONEY-GLAZED
ASPARAGUS (PAGE 23) AND
TURMERIC RICE (PAGE 78) TO
MAKE A COMPLETE MEAL.

Per Serving
Calories: 137; Fat: 2g;
Carbohydrates: 23g;
Fiber: 9g; Protein: 8g;
Sodium: 450mg

This Ethiopian yellow split pea soup is called Yekik Alicha. It's a mainstay in all households. The traditional recipe doesn't call for red bell pepper, but I think it adds robust flavor and a beautiful color to create an even more vibrant dish.

2 teaspoons corn oil

1 yellow onion, finely chopped

2 garlic cloves, finely chopped

1 teaspoon finely chopped
fresh ginger

¼ cup (½-inch pieces) diced
red bell pepper

1½ teaspoons kosher salt

½ teaspoon ground turmeric

1 cup yellow split peas, soaked
for 10 minutes, then drained

3 cups water

Rice or flatbread, for serving

1. **Sauté the onion and garlic.** Select Sauté, and pour in the oil. Once hot, add the onion and garlic and sauté until the onion is translucent, about 5 minutes. Add the ginger and bell pepper, and sauté for 1 minute more. Press Cancel. Mix in the salt, turmeric, yellow split peas, and water.

2. **Pressure cook the yellow peas.** Lock the lid into place. Select Pressure Cook or Manual, and adjust the pressure to High and the time to 15 minutes. Make sure the steam release knob is in the sealed position. After cooking, naturally release the pressure. Unlock and remove the lid. Using a ladle, mash the split peas. Serve hot with rice or any flatbread.

CHANNA MASALA

DAIRY-FREE, GLUTEN-FREE, NUT-FREE, VEGAN

SERVES 6

PREP AND FINISHING: 10 MINUTES, PLUS AT LEAST 8 HOURS TO SOAK

SAUTÉ: 7 MINUTES

PRESSURE COOK: 30 MINUTES ON HIGH

RELEASE: NATURAL

TOTAL TIME: 9 HOURS

PAIR IT: MAKE IT A THREE-COURSE INDIAN MEAL BY PAIRING THIS DISH WITH TURMERIC RICE (PAGE 78) AND INDIAN-STYLE CARROT AND COCONUT KHEER (PAGE 117).

Per Serving
Calories: 166; Fat: 5g; Carbohydrates: 25g; Fiber: 7g; Protein: 8g; Sodium: 150mg

Any self-respecting Indian restaurant menu is incomplete without a Channa Masala, or Chickpea Curry. It's easy to see why this dish is such a national favorite. The flavors of coriander and chili powder blend really well together, and, when combined with chickpeas, it makes such a lovely, fragrant dish.

1 cup dried chickpeas

1 tablespoon corn oil

1 tablespoon cumin seeds

1 (1-inch) cinnamon stick

1 yellow onion, finely chopped

3 tomatoes, finely chopped

1 teaspoon chili powder

2 teaspoons ground coriander

½ teaspoon ground turmeric

½ tablespoon salt

2½ cups water

3 tablespoons finely chopped fresh cilantro, divided

1. Soak the beans. In a large bowl, cover the chickpeas with 2 to 3 inches of cold water. Soak at room temperature for 8 hours, or overnight. Drain and rinse.

2. Sauté the masala. Select Sauté, and pour in the oil. Once hot, add the cumin seeds and cinnamon stick and cook for 30 seconds. Add the onion and sauté until translucent, about 5 minutes. Add the tomatoes, chili powder, coriander, turmeric, and salt. Cook, stirring frequently, until the tomatoes are soft, about 2 minutes. Pour the water into the inner pot, and add the chickpeas and 1½ tablespoons of cilantro.

3. Pressure cook the beans. Lock the lid into place. Select Pressure Cook or Manual, and adjust the pressure to High and the time to 30 minutes. Make sure the steam release knob is in the sealed position. After cooking, naturally release the pressure. Unlock and remove the lid. Stir the curry. Sprinkle the remaining 1½ tablespoons of cilantro on top and serve hot.

NEPALI MIXED BEAN STEW

DAIRY-FREE, GLUTEN-FREE, NUT-FREE, VEGAN

SERVES 8

PREP AND FINISHING: 10 MINUTES, PLUS 2 HOURS TO SOAK

SAUTÉ: 5 + 5 MINUTES

PRESSURE COOK:
30 MINUTES ON HIGH

RELEASE: NATURAL

TOTAL TIME: 3 HOURS

INGREDIENT TIP: ADDING ¼ TO ½ TEASPOON OF CAROM SEEDS TO BEAN-BASED STEWS NOT ONLY ENHANCES THE FLAVOR, BUT THE SEEDS ARE ALSO KNOWN TO HELP AID IN DIGESTION.

Per Serving
Calories: 206; Fat: 3g;
Carbohydrates: 33g;
Fiber: 16g; Protein: 13g;
Sodium: 10mg

This stew is inspired by the popular Nepali dish called Kwati. Traditionally, it's prepared with nine different sprouted bean varieties and served during the Gunla festival. My version calls for a mix of 15 different beans and lentils, but don't worry; you don't have to buy them separately. Any prepackaged bag of dried mixed beans and lentils found in most grocery stores will work here.

2 cups mixed dried beans and lentils

3 teaspoons corn oil, divided

1 yellow onion, roughly chopped

3 garlic cloves

2 teaspoons finely chopped fresh ginger

3 tomatoes, roughly chopped

1 teaspoon fennel seeds

1 teaspoon carom seeds

1 teaspoon cumin seeds

1 teaspoon ground coriander

1 teaspoon chili powder

½ teaspoon ground turmeric

2 cups water

1 tablespoon chopped fresh cilantro

1. Soak the beans and lentils. In a large bowl, cover the beans and lentils with 2 to 3 inches of cold water. Soak at room temperature for 2 hours. Drain and rinse.

2. Sauté the onion and tomato. Select Sauté, and pour in 1½ teaspoons of oil. Once hot, add the onion, garlic, ginger, and tomatoes. Sauté for 5 minutes or until the onion is translucent, stirring occasionally. Press Cancel. Let cool for 5 minutes.

3. Make the onion paste. Transfer the onion mixture to a blender. Blend to make a coarse paste.

4. Sauté the vegetables. Select Sauté, and pour in the remaining 1½ teaspoons of oil. Once hot, add the fennel, carom, and cumin seeds, and sauté for 30 seconds. Add the onion paste, coriander, chili powder, and turmeric. Cook, stirring frequently, for 1 minute. Add the water and deglaze the pan, scraping up any browned bits from the bottom of the pot. Add the beans to the inner pot.

5. Pressure cook the beans and lentils. Lock the lid into place. Press Bean, and adjust the pressure to High and the time to 30 minutes. Make sure the steam release knob is in the sealed position. After cooking, naturally release the pressure. Unlock and remove the lid. Stir in the cilantro and serve hot.

EGYPTIAN-STYLE FAVA BEAN CURRY

DAIRY-FREE, GLUTEN-FREE, NUT-FREE, VEGAN

SERVES 8

PREP AND FINISHING: 10 MINUTES, PLUS AT LEAST 10 HOURS TO SOAK

PRESSURE COOK:
40 MINUTES ON HIGH

RELEASE: NATURAL

SAUTÉ: 10 MINUTES

TOTAL TIME: 11 HOURS

INGREDIENT TIP: DURING THE SPRING SEASON, I ENCOURAGE YOU TO OPT FOR FRESH FAVA BEANS. SHELL THE BEANS FIRST, THEN COOK ON HIGH FOR ABOUT 6 MINUTES.

Per Serving
Calories: 156; Fat: 2g;
Carbohydrates: 26g;
Fiber: 10g; Protein: 11g;
Sodium: 9mg

It's true that the word curry is often associated with Indian cuisine. But around the world, various cultures have different takes on the spice blend, from East Asia to eastern Africa. This version is an Egyptian-style curry made with vitamin- and protein-rich fava beans. Fava beans must be shelled before you eat them, so I always make extra to keep in our refrigerator—they make an easy snack.

2 cups dried fava beans

3 cups water

2 teaspoons corn oil

1 yellow onion, finely chopped

6 garlic cloves, finely chopped

2 serrano chiles, finely chopped

2 tomatoes, finely chopped

1 teaspoon ground cumin

2 teaspoons ground coriander

1 teaspoon dried oregano

2 tablespoons freshly squeezed lemon juice

2 tablespoons finely chopped fresh cilantro

1. Soak the beans. In a large bowl, cover the beans with 2 to 3 inches of cold water. Soak at room temperature for 10 to 12 hours, or overnight. Drain and rinse.

2. Pressure cook the beans. Pour the water into the inner pot, and add the fava beans. Lock the lid into place. Select Pressure Cook or Manual, and adjust the pressure to High and the time to 40 minutes. Make sure the steam release knob is in the sealed position. After cooking, naturally release the pressure. Drain the beans, and rinse with cold water. Wipe the inner pot dry.

3. Peel the fava beans. Peel and discard the skins by squeezing the cooked beans between your thumb and forefinger. The skin should come off easily.

4. Make the curry. Select Sauté, and pour in the oil. Once hot, add the onion, garlic, and chiles, and sauté until the onion is translucent, about 5 minutes. Add the tomatoes, cumin, coriander, and oregano, and stir to combine. Cover and cook for 3 to 4 minutes or until the tomatoes are soft. Add the beans, and cook for 2 minutes more. Press Cancel. Stir in the lemon juice and cilantro, and serve hot.

MIXED-VEGETABLE DAL

SERVES 6

PREP AND FINISHING: 10 MINUTES

SAUTÉ: 5 MINUTES

PRESSURE COOK:
15 MINUTES ON HIGH

RELEASE: NATURAL

TOTAL TIME: 40 MINUTES

INGREDIENT TIP: ANY TYPE OF STURDY VEGETABLE WORKS WELL IN THIS RECIPE, SO FEEL FREE TO EXPERIMENT WITH WHATEVER IS IN SEASON. ALSO, GREEN OR YELLOW LENTILS WORK WELL WHEN MAKING THIS DISH. JUST BE SURE TO INCREASE THE COOK TIME BY 2 TO 3 MINUTES.

Per Serving
Calories: 157; Fat: 3g;
Carbohydrates: 25g;
Fiber: 11g; Protein: 10g;
Sodium: 600mg

Dal, or lentils, are a quintessential part of almost any Indian meal. Every state in India has its own unique version—some with veggies and some without. My version offers a mildly spiced dal and includes seasonal vegetables. It pairs well with rice or any flatbread of your choice.

1 tablespoon butter

1 tablespoon cumin seeds

1 teaspoon finely chopped fresh ginger

2 green Thai chiles, finely chopped

½ cup (1-inch chunks) chopped carrot

½ cup (1-inch cubes) chopped butternut squash

½ cup (1-inch chunks) chopped zucchini

2 cups broccoli florets

2 teaspoons kosher salt

½ teaspoon ground turmeric

¼ teaspoon ground allspice

3 cups water

1 cup red lentils, rinsed and drained

3 tablespoons chopped fresh cilantro

1. **Sauté the onion and garlic.** Select Sauté, and melt the butter. Add the cumin seeds, ginger, and chiles, and sauté for 1 minute. Add the carrot, butternut squash, zucchini, broccoli, salt, turmeric, and allspice, and mix well. Pour the water into the inner pot, and mix in the lentils.

2. **Cook the lentils.** Lock the lid into place. Select Pressure Cook or Manual, and adjust the pressure to High and the time to 15 minutes. Make sure the steam release knob is in the sealed position. After cooking, naturally release the pressure. Unlock and remove the lid.

3. **Finish the dal.** Using the back of a ladle, mash the lentils and vegetables. Stir in the cilantro, and serve hot.

CARIBBEAN-STYLE BEANS AND RICE

DAIRY-FREE, GLUTEN-FREE, NUT-FREE, VEGAN

SERVES 4

PREP AND FINISHING: 15 MINUTES, PLUS 6 HOURS TO SOAK

SAUTÉ: 7 MINUTES

PRESSURE COOK: 10 + 3 MINUTES ON HIGH

RELEASE: NATURAL + NATURAL 5 MINUTES, THEN QUICK

TOTAL TIME: 6 HOURS 50 MINUTES

DOUBLE IT: DOUBLE THE RECIPE BY DOUBLING ALL THE INGREDIENTS, INCLUDING THE WATER, BUT NOT THE COOKING TIME. IF USING A MINI, MAKE SURE YOU DON'T FILL THE POT MORE THAN TWO-THIRDS FULL; OTHERWISE, IT WILL OVERFLOW.

Per Serving
Calories: 329; Fat: 16g;
Carbohydrates: 41g;
Fiber: 5g; Protein: 8g;
Sodium: 450mg

Caribbean cuisine is known for its use of spices and coconut. A traditional recipe for Caribbean beans and rice calls for a very hot Scotch bonnet pepper. My take uses the much milder jalapeño pepper. The coconut milk not only balances the heat, but also makes the rice rich and creamy.

⅓ cup dried kidney beans

2 cups water

1 teaspoon corn oil

1 yellow onion, finely chopped

2 garlic cloves, finely chopped

2 teaspoons seeded and finely chopped jalapeño

1 tomato, finely chopped

1 teaspoon dried thyme

1 teaspoon kosher salt

⅔ cup basmati rice, rinsed and drained

1 cup full-fat coconut milk

1. **Soak the beans.** In a large bowl, cover the kidney beans with 2 to 3 inches of cold water. Soak at room temperature for 6 hours. Drain and rinse.

2. **Pressure cook the beans.** Pour the water into the inner pot, and add the beans. Lock the lid into place. Select Pressure Cook or Manual, and adjust the pressure to High and the time to 10 minutes. Make sure the steam release knob is in the sealed position. After cooking, naturally release the pressure. Unlock and remove the lid. Drain the beans, reserving and setting aside ½ cup of bean water. Wipe the inner pot dry.

3. **Sauté the onion and garlic.** Select Sauté, and pour in the oil. Once hot, add the onion, garlic, and jalapeño, and sauté until the onion is translucent, about 5 minutes Stir in the tomato, thyme, and salt, and cook for 2 minutes.

4. **Pressure cook the rice.** Pour the reserved bean water into the inner pot. Stir in the rice and coconut milk. Lock the lid into place. Select Pressure Cook or Manual, and adjust the pressure to High and the time to 3 minutes. Make sure the steam release knob is in the sealed position. After cooking, naturally release the pressure for 5 minutes, then quick release any remaining pressure. Unlock and remove the lid. Let the rice cool for 5 minutes, then fluff with a fork and serve hot with the beans.

PINTO BEAN AND VEGETABLE TACOS

GLUTEN-FREE, NUT-FREE

SERVES 6

PREP AND FINISHING: 10 MINUTES,
PLUS 4 HOURS TO SOAK

PRESSURE COOK:
8 MINUTES ON HIGH

RELEASE: NATURAL
10 MINUTES, THEN QUICK

SAUTÉ: 12 MINUTES

TOTAL TIME: 4 HOURS 50 MINUTES

INGREDIENT TIP: IF THE TACO
SEASONING IS TOO SPICY FOR
YOUR PALATE, REPLACE IT WITH
1 TEASPOON OF TABASCO SAUCE.

Per Serving
Calories: 277; Fat: 11g;
Carbohydrates: 27g;
Fiber: 6g; Protein: 18g;
Sodium: 987mg

Cooking vegetarian tacos usually means just replacing traditional meat fillings with cooked beans. But my recipe definitely ups the filling game. I've added an abundance of vegetables to give this dish a boost of flavor and texture. Taco Tuesdays never tasted so good.

1 cup dried pinto beans	2 teaspoons kosher salt
2 cups water	1 teaspoon ground cumin
2 tablespoons corn oil	1 teaspoon taco seasoning
1 yellow onion, finely chopped	½ teaspoon chili powder
10 white mushrooms, halved	6 corn tortillas, warmed
¼ cup chopped bell peppers	½ cup Mexican-blend shredded cheese
1 zucchini, cut into 1-inch chunks	1 tablespoon finely chopped fresh cilantro
1 medium carrot, cut into 1-inch chunks	

1. **Soak the beans.** In a large bowl, cover the pinto beans with 2 to 3 inches of cold water. Soak at room temperature for 4 hours. Drain and rinse.

2. **Pressure cook the beans.** Pour the water into the inner pot, and add the beans. Lock the lid into place. Select Pressure Cook or Manual, and adjust the pressure to High and the time to 8 minutes. Make sure the steam release knob is in the sealed position. After cooking, naturally release the pressure for 10 minutes, then quick release any remaining pressure. Drain the beans. Wipe the inner pot dry.

3. **Sauté the vegetables.** Select Sauté, and pour in the oil. Once hot, add the onion and sauté until translucent, about 5 minutes. Add the mushrooms, bell pepper, zucchini, carrot, salt, cumin, taco seasoning, and chili powder. Mix together and cook for 5 minutes, until the bell pepper becomes tender, stirring every 2 minutes. Add the beans, and continue cooking and stirring for another 2 minutes.

4. **Make the Tacos.** Fill the warmed tortillas with the beans and vegetables, garnish with shredded cheese and cilantro, and serve.

THREE-BEAN CHILI

GLUTEN-FREE, NUT-FREE

SERVES 10

PREP AND FINISHING: 10 MINUTES,
PLUS AT LEAST 8 HOURS TO SOAK

SAUTÉ: 10 MINUTES

PRESSURE COOK:
30 MINUTES ON HIGH

RELEASE: NATURAL

TOTAL TIME: 9 HOURS

MAKE IT NEW: MAKE A BEAN CHILI
MAC AND CHEESE. COMBINE THE
CHILI WITH COOKED PASTA, AND
TOP IT WITH CHEESE AND A DASH
OR TWO OF DRIED OREGANO.

Per Serving
Calories: 255; Fat: 4g;
Carbohydrates: 41g;
Fiber: 10g; Protein: 15g;
Sodium: 445mg

Something about fall and winter calls for chili. This hearty Three-Bean Chili is full of flavor. Whether hitting the spot on a cold day or making a batch for Super Bowl game day, it's a crowd-pleaser through and through. Bonus points: It freezes beautifully and can be reheated in no time.

1 cup dried black beans	2 tablespoons ketchup
1 cup dried pinto beans	1 tablespoon dark chili powder
1 cup dried kidney beans	2 teaspoons kosher salt
1 tablespoon corn oil	1 teaspoon ground cumin
1 yellow onion, roughly chopped	1 teaspoon unsweetened cocoa powder
3 garlic cloves, finely chopped	¼ teaspoon smoked paprika
3 Roma tomatoes, finely chopped	¼ teaspoon cayenne pepper
1½ cups finely chopped yellow bell pepper	4½ cups water
	½ cup Mexican-blend shredded cheese, for garnish

1. **Soak the beans.** In a large bowl, cover the black, pinto, and kidney beans with 2 to 3 inches of cold water. Soak at room temperature for 8 hours, or overnight. Drain and rinse.

2. **Sauté the vegetables.** Select Sauté, and pour in the oil. Once hot, add the onion and garlic, and sauté until the onion is translucent, about 5 minutes. Add the tomatoes, and cook until soft, about 5 minutes. Mix in the bell pepper, ketchup, chili powder, salt, cumin, cocoa, paprika, and cayenne pepper.

3. **Pressure cook the beans.** Pour the water into the inner pot, and add the beans. Lock the lid into place. Select Bean/Chili, and adjust the pressure to High and the time to 30 minutes. Make sure the steam release knob is in the sealed position. After cooking, naturally release the pressure. Unlock and remove the lid. Using the back of a wooden spoon, mash some of the beans, and then thoroughly stir the chili. Serve topped with the cheese.

Minestrone

PAGE 67

Chapter Four
SOUPS AND STEWS

TOMATO-BASIL SOUP

GLUTEN-FREE, NUT-FREE

SERVES: 6

PREP AND FINISHING: 15 MINUTES

SAUTÉ: 3 MINUTES

PRESSURE COOK:
5 MINUTES ON HIGH

RELEASE: NATURAL

TOTAL TIME: 35 MINUTES

DOUBLE IT: DOUBLE THE
INGREDIENTS AND THE WATER
AND COOK FOR 8 MINUTES.

Per Serving
Calories: 90; Fat: 6g;
Carbohydrates: 8g;
Fiber: 2g; Protein: 2g;
Sodium: 342mg

Cooking with fresh ingredients always makes any dish more flavorful, and this restaurant-style soup is the perfect example. Best of all, you can prepare it in about 30 minutes. It's my favorite year-round soup to make.

1 tablespoon butter

¼ cup finely chopped onion

3 garlic cloves

6 medium tomatoes, roughly chopped (about 1¾ pounds)

1 cup fresh basil leaves, chopped, divided

1 teaspoon kosher salt

1 teaspoon freshly ground black pepper

¼ teaspoon sugar

2 cups water

¼ cup heavy (whipping) cream

½ cup store-bought croutons, for garnish (optional, omit for gluten-free)

1. **Sauté the vegetables.** Select Sauté, and melt the butter. Add the onion and garlic, and sauté for 1 minute. Add the tomatoes, half of the chopped basil, and the salt, pepper, and sugar. Add the water, and stir to combine.

2. **Pressure cook the tomatoes.** Lock the lid into place. Select Pressure Cook or Manual, and adjust the pressure to High and the time to 5 minutes. Make sure the steam release knob is in the sealed position. After cooking, naturally release the pressure. Unlock and remove the lid. Stir the soup.

3. **Purée the soup.** Using an immersion blender, purée the soup. Stir in the cream and the remaining chopped basil. Serve hot, garnished with the croutons (if desired).

BEET SOUP

GLUTEN-FREE, NUT-FREE

SERVES: 6

PREP AND FINISHING: 10 MINUTES

SAUTÉ: 3 + 5 MINUTES

PRESSURE COOK:
12 MINUTES ON HIGH

RELEASE: NATURAL

TOTAL TIME: 40 MINUTES

MAKE IT VEGAN: REPLACE THE
CREAM WITH $^1/_2$ CUP OF FULL-FAT
COCONUT MILK OR ALMOND MILK.

Per Serving
Calories: 98; Fat: 6g;
Carbohydrates: 10g;
Fiber: 2g; Protein: 2g;
Sodium: 370mg

If you're looking to add more beets to your diet—start here. Vibrant and earthy, my beet soup is loaded with vitamin C. Plus, the bright color and touch of sweetness make for a dramatic presentation—and taste—at the dinner table.

1 tablespoon corn oil

2 shallots, finely chopped

2 garlic cloves, finely chopped

1 pound red beets, peeled and quartered (about 4 medium beets)

1 medium carrot, peeled and cut into bite-size pieces

1 teaspoon kosher salt

1 teaspoon sugar

3 cups water, divided

¼ cup heavy (whipping) cream

1. **Sauté the beets.** Select Sauté, and pour in the oil. Once hot, add the shallots and garlic and cook for 1 minute. Add the beets, carrot, salt, sugar, and 2½ cups of water. Stir to combine.

2. **Pressure cook the beets.** Lock the lid into place. Select Pressure Cook or Manual, and adjust the pressure to High and the time to 12 minutes. Make sure the steam release knob is in the sealed position. After cooking, naturally release the pressure. Unlock and remove the lid.

3. **Purée the vegetables.** Using a slotted spoon, transfer the beets and carrot to a blender. Pour the broth into a medium bowl. Pulse the beets and carrot, while little by little adding 1 cup of broth. Continue blending until you've reached a smooth and silky texture. It will still be thick at this point.

4. **Simmer the soup.** Select Sauté. Pour the puréed beets and any remaining broth into the inner pot, and stir to combine. Use the remaining ½ cup of water to rinse out the blender; pour this into the inner pot. Simmer the soup for 5 minutes. Press Cancel, then stir in the cream. Serve warm.

CURRIED CARROT AND GINGER SOUP

**DAIRY-FREE, GLUTEN-
FREE, NUT-FREE, VEGAN**

SERVES 4

PREP AND FINISHING: 10 MINUTES

SAUTÉ: 3 MINUTES

PRESSURE COOK:
15 MINUTES ON HIGH

RELEASE: NATURAL

TOTAL TIME: 40 MINUTES

PAIR IT: SERVE THIS SOUP
ALONG WITH TURMERIC RICE
(PAGE 78) AND SOME YOGURT
RELISH TO MAKE A SOOTHING
TREAT DURING WINTER.

Per Serving
Calories: 83; Fat: 3g;
Carbohydrates: 13g;
Fiber: 4g; Protein: 2g;
Sodium: 63mg

I love ginger. What's great about this flavorful root is that a small amount goes a long way. It has great medicinal properties, too, including aiding digestion and calming upset stomachs. Here is a soothing carrot soup with the flavors of ginger and curry, perfect for cold winter nights.

2 teaspoons corn oil

2 teaspoons finely chopped fresh ginger

5 large carrots, cut into bite-size pieces

1 teaspoon curry powder

2 tablespoons red lentils, rinsed

2 teaspoons kosher salt

2½ cups water

1. Sauté the vegetables. Select Sauté, and pour in the oil. Once hot, add the ginger and carrots, and sauté for about 2 minutes, until the carrots start to soften. Stir in the curry powder, lentils, salt, and water.

2. Pressure cook the carrots. Lock the lid into place. Select Pressure Cook or Manual, and adjust the pressure to High and the time to 15 minutes. Make sure the steam release knob is in the sealed position. After cooking, naturally release the pressure. Unlock and remove the lid.

3. Purée the soup. Using an immersion blender, purée the soup. Mix thoroughly, and serve hot.

FRESH TOMATO GAZPACHO

DAIRY-FREE, GLUTEN-FREE, NUT-FREE, VEGAN

SERVES 4

PREP AND FINISHING: 5 MINUTES, PLUS AT LEAST 1 HOUR TO CHILL

PRESSURE COOK: 3 MINUTES ON HIGH

RELEASE: QUICK

TOTAL TIME: 1 HOUR 20 MINUTES

DOUBLE IT: YOU CAN DOUBLE THE INGREDIENTS, BUT NOT THE WATER. THE COOK TIME REMAINS THE SAME.

Per Serving
Calories: 50; Fat: 1g;
Carbohydrates: 11g;
Fiber: 3g; Protein: 2g;
Sodium: 450mg

Soup can't get any easier than this. This quick and easy gazpacho recipe made with tomatoes, cucumber, and fresh basil leaves makes the perfect cold summer soup. I like to season mine with cumin and paprika to balance out the acidity of the fresh tomato.

1½ cups water

4 large tomatoes, slit on the top in a cross shape

4 fresh basil leaves, finely chopped

1 teaspoon kosher salt

1 teaspoon sugar

½ teaspoon ground cumin

½ teaspoon paprika

½ teaspoon freshly squeezed lemon juice

1 English cucumber, peeled, seeded, and cut into bite-size chunks

1. Pressure cook the tomatoes. Pour the water into the inner pot, then add the tomatoes. Lock the lid into place. Select Pressure Cook or Manual, and adjust the pressure to High and the cooking time to 3 minutes. Make sure the steam release knob is in the sealed position. After cooking, quick release the pressure.

2. Remove the tomato skin. Unlock and remove the lid. Drain the tomatoes and let cool for 5 minutes. Peel the tomato skin and discard.

3. Assemble the gazpacho. In a blender, combine the tomatoes, basil, salt, sugar, cumin, paprika, and lemon juice, and purée until smooth (or your preferred consistency). Add the cucumber, and pulse the mixture for a chunky gazpacho. Chill for at least for 1 hour before serving.

BUTTERNUT SQUASH COCONUT MILK SOUP

DAIRY-FREE, GLUTEN-FREE, NUT-FREE, VEGAN

SERVES 8

PREP AND FINISHING: 10 MINUTES

SAUTÉ: 5 + 5 MINUTES

PRESSURE COOK:
15 MINUTES ON HIGH

RELEASE: NATURAL

TOTAL TIME: 45 MINUTES

PAIR IT: PAIR THIS MILD SOUP WITH SPICY JOLLOF RICE (PAGE 80) FOR A DELICIOUS MEAL.

Per Serving
Calories: 204; Fat: 14g;
Carbohydrates: 18g;
Fiber: 4g; Protein: 5g;
Sodium: 1,048mg

This is a creamy and rich vegan soup made with the sweet heartiness of butternut squash. The coconut milk adds another layer of creamy texture and richness and takes the flavor to the next level. Serve this at your next dinner party and impress your guests.

1 tablespoon extra-virgin olive oil

½ cup finely chopped onion

2 garlic cloves, finely chopped

2 pounds (1-inch chunks) butternut squash, peeled

3 teaspoons dried oregano

3 teaspoons kosher salt

1 (32-ounce) container vegetable broth

1 (14-ounce) can full-fat coconut milk

1. Sauté the vegetables. Select Sauté, and pour in the oil. Once hot, add the onion and garlic, and sauté until the onion is translucent, about 5 minutes. Stir in the butternut squash, oregano, and salt. Add the broth.

2. Pressure cook the butternut squash. Lock the lid into place. Select Pressure Cook or Manual, and adjust the pressure to High and the time to 15 minutes. Make sure the steam release knob is in the sealed position. After cooking, naturally release the pressure.

3. Purée the soup. Unlock and remove the lid. Using an immersion blender, purée the soup. Select Sauté, and stir in the coconut milk. Simmer the soup for 5 minutes. Serve hot.

FRENCH ONION SOUP

NUT-FREE

SERVES 8

PREP AND FINISHING: 15 MINUTES

SAUTÉ: 25 MINUTES

PRESSURE COOK:
10 MINUTES ON HIGH

RELEASE: QUICK

BAKE: 20 MINUTES

TOTAL TIME: 1 HOUR 20 MINUTES

INGREDIENT TIP: USE DRY
WHITE WINE OR SHERRY
VINEGAR INSTEAD OF APPLE
CIDER VINEGAR TO DEGLAZE
THE POT. THE ALCOHOL BURNS
AWAY BUT PRODUCES A
DEEP, AROMATIC FLAVOR.

Per Serving
Calories: 332; Fat: 15g;
Carbohydrates: 36g;
Fiber: 3g; Protein: 14g;
Sodium: 950mg

Many may assume that this classic soup is vegetarian, yet traditional recipes call for using beef broth. My version omits the beef broth but none of the depth and flavor. So, go ahead and wow your guests with this delicious vegetarian version of the classic cheesy French onion soup—they'll be hard pressed to resist it.

3 tablespoons butter

2 pounds yellow onions, thinly sliced

¼ cup sugar

2 teaspoons kosher salt

2 tablespoons apple cider vinegar

1 (32-ounce) container vegetable broth

1 tablespoon dried thyme

2 dried bay leaves

1 tablespoon vegan Worcestershire sauce

8 slices rustic bread

2 cups shredded Cheddar cheese

1. Caramelize the onion. Select Sauté, and adjust to keep it in the More setting. Melt the butter, and add the onions, sugar, and salt. Cook for about 25 minutes, stirring every 3 minutes, until the onions are a deep brown.

2. Deglaze the pan. Add the vinegar, and deglaze the pot, scraping up any browned bits from the bottom. Stir in the broth, thyme, bay leaves, and Worcestershire sauce.

3. Preheat the oven to 375˚.

4. Pressure cook the soup. Lock the lid into place. Select Pressure Cook or Manual, and adjust the pressure to High and the time to 10 minutes. Make sure the steam release knob is in the sealed position. After cooking, quick release the pressure. Carefully open the lid and mix.

5. Assemble the soup. Ladle the soup into oven-safe ramekins or soup bowls. Top each with a bread slice and the cheese.

6. Bake. Bake for 20 minutes or until the cheese melts. Remove the bay leaves, and serve hot.

CREAM OF ASPARAGUS SOUP

GLUTEN-FREE, NUT-FREE

SERVES 6

PREP AND FINISHING: 25 MINUTES

SAUTÉ: 12 MINUTES

PRESSURE COOK:
4 MINUTES ON HIGH

RELEASE: NATURAL

TOTAL TIME: 50 MINUTES

TRY THIS: THIS RECIPE WORKS WELL FOR A VARIETY OF DIFFERENT VEGETABLES, INCLUDING BROCCOLI, CAULIFLOWER, AND MUSHROOMS. FOR BROCCOLI OR CAULIFLOWER, INCREASE THE COOK TIME TO 8 MINUTES; FOR MUSHROOMS DECREASE THE COOK TIME TO 4 MINUTES. PRESSURE REMAINS THE SAME.

Per Serving
Calories: 254; Fat: 18g;
Carbohydrates: 19g;
Fiber: 9g; Protein: 11g;
Sodium: 829mg

I always thought cream of asparagus soup sounded like a labor-intensive effort. But once I started using my Instant Pot®, those preconceived notions melted away. Not only is this soup super easy to make, but it's also rich and creamy and a good source of vitamins A, C, and E.

1 tablespoon salted butter

½ cup finely chopped onion

3 garlic cloves, finely chopped

1½ pounds asparagus (approximately 2 bunches or 25 single stalks), woody stems trimmed, cut into 1-inch pieces

2 teaspoons kosher salt

1 teaspoon freshly ground black pepper

1½ cups vegetable broth

1 cup heavy (whipping) cream

1. **Sauté the asparagus.** Select Sauté, and melt the butter. Add the onion and garlic, and cook until the onion is translucent, about 5 minutes. Add the asparagus, salt, pepper, and broth. Continue cooking, stirring frequently, for 6 to 7 minutes or until the asparagus is soft.

2. **Pressure cook the soup.** Lock the lid into place. Select Pressure Cook or Manual, and adjust the pressure to High and the time to 4 minutes. Make sure the steam release knob is in the sealed position. After cooking, naturally release the pressure.

3. **Purée the soup.** Unlock and remove the lid. Using an immersion blender, purée the soup. Add the cream, and mix thoroughly. Cover with the lid, and leave the Instant Pot® in Keep Warm mode for at least 15 minutes. Serve hot.

BROCCOLI-CHEDDAR SOUP

NUT-FREE

SERVES 6

PREP AND FINISHING: 25 MINUTES

SAUTÉ: 3 MINUTES

PRESSURE COOK:
5 MINUTES ON HIGH

RELEASE: NATURAL

TOTAL TIME: 45 MINUTES

MAKE IT GLUTEN-FREE: SKIP THE SLURRY TO MAKE IT GLUTEN-FREE. SIMPLY ADD AN EXTRA ¼ CUP OF CREAM CHEESE TO THE SOUP TO HELP THICKEN IT.

Per Serving
Calories: 278; Fat: 24g;
Carbohydrates: 8g;
Fiber: 2g; Protein: 9g;
Sodium: 425mg

Nothing warms the heart like a bowl of broccoli-Cheddar soup. It's not just a decadent, rich soup. It's also a great way to sneak some dark green vegetables into your diet. Even the kids won't mind eating their broccoli when it's served in a cheesy bowl.

1 tablespoon salted butter

1 yellow onion, finely chopped

1 garlic clove, finely chopped

½ cup grated carrot

2½ cups broccoli florets

2 cups vegetable broth

1 cup plus 3 tablespoons water, divided

1 cup heavy (whipping) cream

1 tablespoon cream cheese

1 cup shredded Cheddar cheese

1 tablespoon all-purpose flour

1. **Sauté the vegetables.** Select Sauté, and melt the butter. Add the onion and garlic, and cook until the onion is translucent, about 5 minutes. Add the carrot, broccoli, broth, and 1 cup of water.

2. **Pressure cook the vegetables.** Lock the lid into place. Select Pressure Cook or Manual, and adjust the pressure to High and the time to 5 minutes. Make sure the steam release knob is in the sealed position. After cooking, naturally release the pressure.

3. **Assemble the soup.** Unlock and remove the lid. Using a potato masher, break up the broccoli into smaller chunks. Select Sauté, and add the cream, cream cheese, and cheese. Stir for about 3 minutes, until the cheese melts. In a small bowl, mix the flour with the remaining 3 tablespoons of water until smooth. Add this slurry to the soup, and stir for 2 minutes. Press Cancel. Cover with the lid, and leave the Instant Pot® in Keep Warm mode for at least 15 minutes before serving.

CORN AND POTATO CHOWDER

DAIRY-FREE, GLUTEN-FREE, NUT-FREE, VEGAN

SERVES 6

PREP AND FINISHING: 10 MINUTES

PRESSURE COOK:
12 MINUTES ON HIGH

RELEASE: NATURAL

TOTAL TIME: 30 MINUTES

MAKE IT NEW: THIS CHOWDER WORKS GREAT AS A PASTA SAUCE, TOO. SIMPLY ADD SOME CORN CHOWDER TO COOKED PASTA, AND TOP IT WITH CHEDDAR OR PARMESAN CHEESE AND A SPRINKLE OF DRIED OREGANO.

Per Serving
Calories: 100; Fat: 0g;
Carbohydrates: 23g; Fiber: 4g;
Protein: 3g; Sodium: 608mg

Rich and silky, this chowder doesn't have any cream in it, but you'd never know—and you won't miss it. This recipe is what the Instant Pot® was made for—just add the ingredients, then sit back and relax. The machine does all the work for you.

4 potatoes, peeled and cubed (about 1½ pounds)

Kernels from 2 ears of corn (approximately 1½ cups)

2 teaspoons dried thyme

2 teaspoons freshly ground black pepper

2 teaspoons kosher salt

1 teaspoon onion powder

3½ cups water

1. Pressure cook the potatoes and corn. In the inner pot, combine the potatoes, corn, thyme, pepper, salt, onion powder, and water. Lock the lid into place. Select Pressure Cook or Manual, and adjust the pressure to High and the time to 12 minutes. Make sure the steam release knob is in the sealed position. After cooking, naturally release the pressure. Unlock and remove the lid. Stir the soup.

2. Purée the soup. Using an immersion blender, purée the soup. Serve hot.

MINESTRONE

DAIRY-FREE, NUT-FREE, VEGAN

SERVES 8

PREP AND FINISHING: 10 MINUTES,
PLUS AT LEAST 8 HOURS TO SOAK

PRESSURE COOK: 8 + 20 +
5 MINUTES ON HIGH

SAUTÉ: 10 MINUTES

RELEASE: NATURAL 5 MINUTES,
THEN QUICK + NATURAL + QUICK

TOTAL TIME: 9 HOURS 10 MINUTES

MAKE IT GLUTEN-FREE: PASTA
IS A STAPLE IN TRADITIONAL
MINESTRONE RECIPES, BUT IF
YOU FOLLOW A GLUTEN-FREE
DIET, YOU CAN OPT FOR A RICE
PASTA OR SKIP IT ALTOGETHER.

Per Serving
Calories: 243; Fat: 3g;
Carbohydrates: 44g;
Fiber: 9g; Protein: 13g;
Sodium: 554mg

Classic minestrone is a longtime favorite. My version doesn't use canned beans or deviate much from traditional recipes, except in the reduced cooking time—thanks to the Instant Pot®. Loaded with beans, fresh vegetables, and pasta, this soup is perfect for lunch or dinner.

1 cup dried kidney beans

½ cup dried navy beans

4 cups water, divided

1 tablespoon extra-virgin olive oil

3 shallots, finely chopped

2 garlic cloves, finely chopped

1 zucchini, cut into bite-size pieces

2 celery stalks, cut into bite-size pieces

1 medium carrot, cut into bite-size pieces

5 white mushrooms, quartered

2 teaspoons kosher salt

2 teaspoons chopped fresh basil, divided

1 teaspoon dried basil

1 teaspoon dried oregano

1 teaspoon freshly ground black pepper

1 cup vegetable broth

1 cup shell pasta

1. Soak the beans. In a large bowl, cover the kidney and navy beans with 2 to 3 inches of cold water. Soak at room temperature for 8 hours, or overnight. Drain and rinse.

2. Pressure cook the beans. Pour 3 cups of water into the inner pot, and add the beans. Lock the lid into place. Select Pressure Cook or Manual, and adjust the pressure to High and the time to 8 minutes. Make sure the steam release knob is in the sealed position. After cooking, naturally release the pressure for 5 minutes, then quick release any remaining pressure. Unlock and remove the lid. Drain the beans, reserving 1 cup of bean water. Wipe the inner pot dry.

3. Sauté the vegetables. Select Sauté, and pour in the oil. Once hot, add the shallots and garlic and cook for 2 minutes. Add the zucchini, celery, carrot, and mushrooms, and sauté for 1 minute. Add the salt, 1 teaspoon of fresh basil, and the dried basil, oregano, and pepper. Stir to combine. Add the 1 cup of bean water and the vegetable broth.

4. Pressure cook the vegetables. Lock the lid into place. Select Soup, and adjust the pressure to High and the time to 20 minutes. Make sure the steam release knob is in the sealed position. After cooking, naturally release the pressure. Unlock and remove the lid.

5. Pressure cook the pasta. Add the pasta, the cooked beans, and the remaining 1 cup of water to the pot. Lock the lid into place. Select Pressure Cook or Manual, and adjust the pressure to High and the time to 5 minutes. Make sure the steam release knob is in the sealed position. After cooking, quick release the pressure.

6. Finish the soup. Unlock and remove the lid. Stir in the remaining fresh basil, and serve hot.

RATATOUILLE

DAIRY-FREE, GLUTEN-FREE, NUT-FREE, VEGAN

SERVES 8

PREP AND FINISHING: 5 MINUTES

SAUTÉ: 7 MINUTES

PRESSURE COOK:
10 MINUTES ON HIGH

RELEASE: NATURAL
3 MINUTES, THEN QUICK

TOTAL TIME: 42 MINUTES

MAKE IT A MEAL: PAIR THIS DISH WITH COUSCOUS SALAD WITH CUCUMBER, OLIVES, AND CARROT (PAGE 101) FOR A COMPLETE MEAL.

Per Serving
Calories: 90; Fat: 3g;
Carbohydrates: 14g; Fiber: 4g;
Protein: 2g; Sodium: 599mg

Ratatouille, the popular French Provençal dish—not the animated movie about a rat that loves to cook—is traditionally a labor-intensive dish to prepare. In my easy version, the squash and bell pepper balance the tartness of the tomatoes and add a bit of sweetness.

2 tablespoons extra-virgin olive oil

3 garlic cloves, finely chopped

1 medium onion, cut into ¼ inch slices

2 small zucchini, cut into ¼ inch slices

1 small eggplant, cut into ¼ inch slices

1 yellow bell pepper, cut into ¼ inch slices

1 small butternut squash, peeled and cut into ¼ inch slices

3 teaspoons dried thyme

10 fresh basil leaves, finely chopped

2 teaspoons kosher salt

1 teaspoon freshly ground black pepper

3 medium tomatoes, cut into ¼ inch slices

3 cups vegetable broth

1. Sauté the garlic and onion. Select Sauté and pour in the olive oil. Once hot, add the garlic and onion and sauté for about 5 minutes.

2. Sauté the vegetables. Add the zucchini, eggplant, bell pepper, butternut squash, thyme, basil, salt, and pepper. Sauté for another 4 minutes. Transfer the vegetables to a tray, and set aside until cool to the touch.

3. Arrange the vegetables. Using an 8-inch round, 2-inch deep ceramic dish, arrange the sautéed vegetables and tomatoes in a pattern. Alternately, place the slices upright, along the edge, until the pan is covered.

4. Pressure cook the vegetables. Place the dish inside the Instant Pot®. Pour the broth over the vegetables. Lock the lid into place. Select Pressure Cook or Manual. Adjust the pressure to High and the time to 10 minutes. Make sure the steam release knob is in the sealed position. After cooking, quick release any remaining pressure.

5. Remove the pan. Carefully remove the pan from the pressure cooker and serve immediately.

QUINOA AND VEGETABLE STEW

DAIRY-FREE, GLUTEN-
FREE, NUT-FREE, VEGAN

SERVES 4

PREP AND FINISHING: 10 MINUTES

SAUTÉ: 5 MINUTES

PRESSURE COOK:
8 MINUTES ON HIGH

RELEASE: NATURAL

TOTAL TIME: 35 MINUTES

TRY THIS: INSTEAD OF QUINOA, TRY ¼ CUP OF BULGUR WHEAT OR COUSCOUS. THEY BOTH ADD TEXTURE AND FIBER TO THE DISH (BUT AREN'T GLUTEN-FREE). WHEN USING EITHER, REDUCE THE COOK TIME TO 2 TO 4 MINUTES. PRESSURE REMAINS THE SAME.

Per Serving
Calories: 196; Fat: 6g;
Carbohydrates: 28g;
Fiber: 6g; Protein: 16g;
Sodium: 1,550mg

This stew of seasonal summer vegetables and quinoa is spiced up with coriander and cumin. It's both nutritious and filling, thanks to generous amounts of fiber. Hearty enough to stand alone, this quinoa stew is an easy-to-create one-pot meal.

2 teaspoons corn oil

1 yellow onion, finely chopped

3 Roma tomatoes, finely chopped

½ cup chopped red bell pepper

1½ cups broccoli florets

1 zucchini, cut into 1-inch chunks

¼ cup frozen corn kernels, thawed to room temperature

¼ cup (½-inch pieces) diced carrot

½ cup quinoa, rinsed

2 teaspoons kosher salt

1 teaspoon ground coriander

½ teaspoon paprika

½ teaspoon ground cumin

1 (32-ounce) container vegetable broth

4 tablespoons finely chopped fresh cilantro, divided

1. **Sauté the vegetables.** Select Sauté, and pour in the oil. Once hot, add the onion, and cook until the onion is translucent, about 5 minutes. Add the tomatoes, bell pepper, broccoli, zucchini, corn, and carrot, and mix well. Add the quinoa, salt, coriander, paprika, cumin, and broth. Add 2 tablespoons of cilantro, and mix thoroughly.

2. **Pressure cook the quinoa.** Lock the lid into place. Select Pressure Cook or Manual, and adjust the pressure to High and the time to 8 minutes. Make sure the steam release knob is in the sealed position. After cooking, naturally release the pressure. Unlock and remove the lid. Stir in the remaining 2 tablespoons of cilantro, and serve hot.

TUSCAN KALE AND POTATO SOUP

SERVES 6

PREP AND FINISHING: 10 MINUTES

SAUTÉ: 10 MINUTES

PRESSURE COOK:
30 MINUTES ON HIGH

RELEASE: NATURAL

TOTAL TIME: 1 HOUR

INGREDIENT TIP: INSTEAD OF KALE, YOU CAN USE SPINACH OR A MIX OF BOTH. FOR AN INTERESTING TAKE ON THIS SOUP, USE SWEET POTATOES INSTEAD OF REGULAR POTATOES. THEY ADD A HINT OF SWEETNESS, BUT NOT SO MUCH THAT IT OVERWHELMS THE SOUP. COOK TIME AND PRESSURE REMAIN THE SAME.

Per Serving
Calories: 186; Fat: 5g;
Carbohydrates: 28g;
Fiber: 5g; Protein: 7g;
Sodium: 1,414mg

Usually, kale soup calls for pork sausage. But I think my vegetarian version really gives the herbs—fennel seeds, basil, garlic, oregano, and, of course, rosemary—a chance to shine through without being overpowered by the meat. I made sure to use the same seasonings you'd find in a traditional pork sausage, so you get all the rich flavor without the extra calories.

2 tablespoons extra-virgin olive oil

1 yellow onion, finely chopped

4 garlic cloves, finely chopped

½ teaspoon fennel seeds

10 ounces baby kale, roughly chopped

3 teaspoons kosher salt

2 teaspoons freshly ground black pepper

1½ teaspoons dried rosemary

1 teaspoon dried oregano

1 teaspoon dried basil

1½ pounds potatoes, peeled and cubed

1 medium carrot, cut into 1-inch chunks

2 celery stalks, cut into 1-inch chunks

1 (32-ounce) container vegetable broth

1. **Sauté the vegetables.** Select Sauté, and pour in the oil. Once hot, add the onion, garlic, and fennel seeds, and cook until the onion is translucent, about 5 minutes. Add the kale, salt, pepper, rosemary, oregano, and basil. Sauté until the kale wilts, about 5 minutes. Add the potatoes, carrot, celery, and broth, and mix well.

2. **Pressure cook the vegetables.** Lock the lid into place. Select Pressure Cook or Manual, and adjust the pressure to High and the time to 30 minutes. Make sure the steam release knob is in the sealed position. After cooking, naturally release the pressure.

3. **Finish the soup.** Unlock and remove the lid. Using a potato masher, roughly mash the potatoes. This helps to thicken the soup. Mix thoroughly, and serve hot.

VEGETARIAN PHO

DAIRY-FREE, NUT-FREE, VEGAN

SERVES 6

PREP AND FINISHING: 15 MINUTES

SAUTÉ: 10 MINUTES

PRESSURE COOK:
40 MINUTES ON HIGH

RELEASE: NATURAL

TOTAL TIME: 1 HOUR 15 MINUTES

MAKE IT GLUTEN-FREE:
USE TAMARI IN PLACE OF THE
SOY SAUCE (MAKE SURE THE
LABEL SAYS GLUTEN-FREE).

Per Serving
Calories: 161; Fat: 4g;
Carbohydrates: 29g;
Fiber: 1g; Protein: 4g;
Sodium: 707mg

Vietnamese pho is all about building soul-satisfying flavors. This spicy broth is laden with rice noodles, tofu, sprouts, and other goodies. This broth uses a bounty of ingredients, but it also works really well as a base for other soups, such as Tibetan-Style Vegetable Noodle Soup (page 74, where you can use it in place of vegetable broth). You'll find that it really intensifies the flavor of the soup, so it's worth the time and effort.

1 tablespoon corn oil

1 bunch scallions, white parts only, coarsely chopped

2 garlic cloves, finely chopped

5 white mushrooms, halved

2 teaspoons finely chopped fresh ginger

1 tablespoon thinly sliced lemongrass

1 (1-inch) cinnamon stick

1 dried bay leaf

3 star anise pods

3 cardamom seeds

3 whole cloves

1 tablespoon coriander seeds

1 teaspoon fennel seeds

1 tablespoon sugar

2 teaspoons kosher salt

1 teaspoon soy sauce, plus more for flavor

4 cups water

6 ounces rice noodles

4 ounces extra-firm tofu, cubed

Sprouts, for garnish

Fresh basil leaves, for garnish

Jalapeños, seeded and cut into rounds, for garnish

Sriracha, for garnish

1. **Prepare the broth.** Select Sauté, and pour in the oil. Once hot, add the scallions, garlic, mushrooms, and ginger, and sauté for 2 minutes or until the mushrooms shrink. Add the lemongrass, cinnamon, bay leaf, star anise, cardamom, cloves, coriander seeds, fennel seeds, sugar, salt, and soy sauce, and mix well. Add the water, and mix again.

2. **Pressure cook the pho, and cook the rice noodles.** Lock the lid into place. Select Pressure Cook or Manual, and adjust the pressure to High and the time to 40 minutes. Make sure the steam release knob is in the sealed position. About 10 minutes before the pho is done cooking, cook the rice noodles according to package directions. After cooking the pho, naturally release the pressure.

3. **Assemble the Pho.** Unlock and remove the lid. Using a fine mesh strainer, strain the broth, discarding the vegetables and spices. Divide the noodles among bowls. Add broth to each, and top each with tofu, sprouts, and basil. Drizzle with additional soy sauce and Sriracha, and serve hot.

TIBETAN-STYLE VEGETABLE NOODLE SOUP

DAIRY-FREE, NUT-FREE, VEGAN

SERVES 6

PREP AND FINISHING: 10 MINUTES

SAUTÉ: 6 MINUTES

PRESSURE COOK:
3 MINUTES ON HIGH

RELEASE: NATURAL
5 MINUTES, THEN QUICK

TOTAL TIME: 35 MINUTES

MAKE IT GLUTEN-FREE: YOU CAN USE RICE NOODLES OR SKIP THE NOODLES ALTOGETHER AND USE TAMARI SAUCE IN PLACE OF SOY SAUCE TO MAKE THIS DISH GLUTEN-FREE (MAKE SURE THE LABEL SAYS GLUTEN-FREE).

Per Serving
Calories: 162; Fat: 6g;
Carbohydrates: 23g;
Fiber: 4g; Protein: 7g;
Sodium: 901mg

I love a dense soup loaded with vegetables and carbs, and this Tibetan-style noodle soup hits the spot. Called Thukpa, this soup is often made with chicken; my version omits the meat, but you still get that rich, hearty flavor.

5 ounces wheat noodles

1 cup water

2 tablespoons corn oil

2 shallots, finely chopped

2 garlic cloves, finely chopped

1 bunch scallions, finely chopped, white and green parts separated

½ cup shredded green cabbage

½ cup grated carrot

½ cup finely chopped mushrooms

1 teaspoon curry powder

2 teaspoons soy sauce

1 teaspoon Sriracha

2 teaspoons sugar

1 teaspoon kosher salt

1 (32-ounce) container vegetable broth

1. Soak the noodles. In a medium bowl, soak the noodles in the water for 5 minutes. Drain.

2. Sauté the vegetables. Select Sauté, and pour in the oil. Once hot, add the shallots, garlic, and white parts of the scallions, and cook for 2 minutes. Add the cabbage, carrot, mushrooms, curry powder, soy sauce, Sriracha, sugar, and salt. Mix well, and cook for 3 to 4 minutes. Add the noodles and the vegetable broth.

3. Pressure cook the vegetables. Lock the lid into place. Select Pressure Cook or Manual, and adjust the pressure to High and the time to 3 minutes. Make sure the steam release knob is in the sealed position. After cooking, naturally release the pressure for 5 minutes, then quick release any remaining pressure. Unlock and remove the lid. Stir the soup well, and serve hot.

MIDDLE EASTERN LENTIL SOUP

**DAIRY-FREE, GLUTEN-
FREE, NUT-FREE, VEGAN**

SERVES 4

PREP AND FINISHING: 10 MINUTES

PRESSURE COOK:
10 MINUTES ON HIGH

RELEASE: NATURAL

SAUTÉ: 10 MINUTES

TOTAL TIME: 40 MINUTES

MAKE IT A MEAL: PAIR WITH
ZA'ATAR-SPICED BULGUR
WHEAT SALAD (PAGE 106)
FOR A COMPLETE MEAL.

Per Serving
Calories: 58; Fat: 1g;
Carbohydrates: 10g;
Fiber: 2g; Protein: 4g;
Sodium: 456mg

Any Middle Eastern meal is incomplete without this much-loved soup. Known as Shorbat Adas, this soup is simple yet delightful. It's made with red lentils and the flavors of cumin, garlic, and parsley.

2½ cups water, divided

½ cup red lentils, rinsed and drained

2 garlic cloves, finely chopped

½ cup finely chopped onion

1 teaspoon freshly ground black pepper

½ teaspoon ground turmeric

½ teaspoon ground cumin

1 teaspoon kosher salt

¼ cup chopped fresh parsley

2 tablespoons freshly squeezed lemon juice

1. **Cook the lentils.** Pour 1½ cups of water into the inner pot, and add the lentils, garlic, and onion. Lock the lid into place. Select Pressure Cook or Manual, and adjust the pressure to High and the time to 10 minutes. Make sure the steam release knob is in the sealed position. After cooking, naturally release the pressure.

2. **Purée the lentils.** Unlock and remove the lid. Using a potato masher, thoroughly mash the lentils.

3. **Finish the soup.** Select Sauté, and add the pepper, turmeric, cumin, salt, and parsley. Mix well, and stir in the remaining 1 cup of water. Simmer for 10 minutes. Press Cancel, and stir in the lemon juice. Serve hot.

*Thai Pineapple
Fried Rice*

PAGE 81

Chapter Five
RICE AND PASTA

TURMERIC RICE

GLUTEN-FREE, NUT-FREE

SERVES 4

PREP AND FINISHING: 5 MINUTES,
PLUS 15 MINUTES TO COOL

SAUTÉ: 1 MINUTE

PRESSURE COOK:
12 MINUTES ON LOW

RELEASE: NATURAL

TOTAL TIME: 45 MINUTES

PAIR IT: YOU CAN SERVE THIS RICE
WITH CHICKPEA CURRY (PAGE 47),
MIXED-VEGETABLE DAL (PAGE 52),
OR ETHIOPIAN-STYLE VEGETABLE
CURRY (PAGE 26). MIXED-
VEGETABLE KORMA (PAGE 32)
ALSO PAIRS WELL WITH THIS RICE.

Per Serving
Calories: 202; Fat: 4g;
Carbohydrates: 38g; Fiber: 1g;
Protein: 4g; Sodium: 151mg

Mild yet fragrant, turmeric is an excellent addition to
any dish. It's known for its antibacterial, antifungal, and
antiseptic properties. You can get the goodness of turmeric
by including its powder form in curries, rice, and soups.
I know this turmeric rice recipe is destined to be one of
your favorites.

1 tablespoon butter

2 dried bay leaves

1 (½-inch) cinnamon stick

1 tablespoon cumin seeds

1 cup basmati rice, rinsed

1¼ cups water

½ teaspoon ground turmeric

½ teaspoon freshly ground
black pepper

½ teaspoon kosher salt

1. Sauté the spices. Select Sauté, and melt the butter. Add
the bay leaves, cinnamon stick, and cumin seeds, and sauté
for 45 to 60 seconds. Add the rice, water, turmeric, pepper,
and salt, and mix well.

2. Pressure cook the rice. Lock the lid into place. Select
Rice. Make sure the steam release knob is in the sealed position. After cooking, naturally release the pressure. Unlock
and remove the lid. Let the rice cool for 15 minutes. Remove
the bay leaves, fluff the rice with a fork, and serve hot.

CILANTRO-LIME RICE

DAIRY-FREE, GLUTEN-FREE, NUT-FREE, VEGAN

....

SERVES 4

PREP AND FINISHING: 5 MINUTES

SAUTÉ: 5 MINUTES

PRESSURE COOK:
25 MINUTES ON HIGH

RELEASE: NATURAL

TOTAL TIME: 45 MINUTES

....

MAKE IT NEW: ADD THIS RICE TO YOUR REFRIED BEANS (PAGE 43) OR PINTO BEAN AND VEGETABLE TACOS (PAGE 54) FOR AN INTERESTING TWIST ON A BURRITO BOWL. TOP WITH SHREDDED LETTUCE, A DOLLOP OF SOUR CREAM, AND SOME CHOPPED TOMATOES, AND YOU'RE READY TO GO.

....

Per Serving
Calories: 206; Fat: 5g;
Carbohydrates: 37g;
Fiber: 2g; Protein: 4g;
Sodium: 128mg

Cilantro and lime are mainstays of Latin and Caribbean cooking, both in the home and in restaurants. My version of this refreshingly flavored rice won't disappoint. I like to make it with brown rice for the added fiber. The cilantro and lime hold up really well against the hearty grain.

1 tablespoon extra-virgin olive oil

2 shallots, chopped

1 cup brown rice, rinsed

1⅓ cups water

½ teaspoon kosher salt

1 tablespoon freshly squeezed lime juice

1 teaspoon grated lime zest

¼ cup finely chopped fresh cilantro

1. Sauté the shallots. Select Sauté, and pour in the oil. Once hot, add the shallots and cook for 45 seconds. Add the rice, water, and salt. Mix well.

2. Pressure cook the rice. Lock the lid into place. Select Pressure Cook or Manual, and adjust the pressure to High and the time to 25 minutes. Make sure the steam release knob is in the sealed position. After cooking, naturally release the pressure.

3. Finish the rice. Unlock and remove the lid. Let the rice cool for 10 minutes. Using a fork, fluff the rice. Stir in the lime juice and zest and the cilantro, and serve hot.

JOLLOF RICE

DAIRY-FREE, GLUTEN-FREE, NUT-FREE, VEGAN

SERVES 4

PREP AND FINISHING: 10 MINUTES, PLUS 15 MINUTES TO COOL

SAUTÉ: 6 MINUTES

PRESSURE COOK:
12 MINUTES ON LOW

RELEASE: NATURAL

TOTAL TIME: 50 MINUTES

DOUBLE IT: YOU CAN DOUBLE THE INGREDIENTS, INCLUDING THE WATER. BE SURE TO COOK THE RICE USING THE RICE PRESET.

Per Serving
Calories: 434; Fat: 4g;
Carbohydrates: 90g;
Fiber: 4g; Protein: 8g;
Sodium: 675mg

Jollof Rice is a staple dish from West Africa. Each country has their own unique version, complete with signature spices, but they all use Scotch bonnet peppers. My version includes vegetables spiced with jalapeños and curry powder. It's a one-pot dish because the rice cooks in the tomato juice and spicy sauce, soaking up all the wonderful, aromatic flavors.

1 tablespoon corn oil

2 dried bay leaves

1 onion, finely chopped

2 garlic cloves, finely chopped

1 teaspoon finely chopped fresh ginger

1 jalapeño, seeded and finely chopped

2 tomatoes, coarsely chopped

2 tablespoons tomato paste

1½ teaspoons kosher salt

1 teaspoon paprika

½ teaspoon curry powder

1 cup chopped carrots

1 cup cauliflower florets (7 or 8 florets)

1 cup short-grain white rice, rinsed

2 cups water

1. Prepare the tomato sauce. Select Sauté, and pour in the corn oil. Once hot, add the bay leaves, onion, garlic, ginger, and jalapeños, and sauté for 5 minutes or until the onion is translucent. Stir in the tomatoes, tomato paste, and salt. Loosely place the lid on top, and cook for 3 minutes or until the tomatoes are soft. Mix in the paprika and curry powder, then stir in the carrots and cauliflower. Add the rice and water, and mix well.

2. Pressure cook the rice. Lock the lid into place. Select Rice. Make sure the steam release knob is in the sealed position. After cooking, naturally release the pressure. Unlock and remove the lid. Let the rice cool for 15 minutes. Remove the bay leaves. Using a fork, gently fluff the rice. Serve hot.

THAI PINEAPPLE FRIED RICE

DAIRY-FREE, VEGAN

SERVES 4

PREP AND FINISHING: 10 MINUTES,
PLUS 15 MINUTES TO COOL

SAUTÉ: 5 MINUTES

PRESSURE COOK:
3 MINUTES ON HIGH

RELEASE: NATURAL
3 MINUTES, THEN QUICK

TOTAL TIME: 45 MINUTES

MAKE IT GLUTEN-FREE: USE
TAMARI SAUCE INSTEAD OF
SOY SAUCE (MAKE SURE THE
LABEL SAYS GLUTEN-FREE).

Per Serving
Calories: 167; Fat: 7g;
Carbohydrates: 24g;
Fiber: 1g; Protein: 3g;
Sodium: 458mg

This fried rice is quite popular in Thai restaurants. The mix of sweet pineapple and savory cashews is irresistible. I like to make mine with leftover or day-old rice. That extra time in the refrigerator allows for the rice to dry out a bit, and the firmer texture makes it ideal for making fried rice. When paired with Thai-Style Vegetable Curry (page 30), it is hard to stick with a single serving.

1 tablespoon corn oil

3 tablespoons cashews

¼ cup finely chopped onion

¼ cup finely chopped scallions, white parts only

2 green Thai chiles, finely chopped

1 cup canned pineapple chunks

4 tablespoons roughly chopped fresh basil leaves, divided

½ teaspoon curry powder

¼ teaspoon ground turmeric

2 teaspoons soy sauce

1 teaspoon kosher salt

1 cup steamed short-grain white rice, preferably a day old

1¼ cups water

1. Sauté the vegetables and pineapple. Select Sauté, and pour in the oil. Once hot, add the cashews and stir for 1 minute. Add the onion, scallions, and chiles, and sauté for 3 to 4 minutes, until the onion is translucent. Mix in the pineapple, 2 tablespoons of basil, and the curry powder, turmeric, soy sauce, and salt. Add the rice and water, and mix again.

2. Pressure cook the rice. Lock the lid into place. Select Pressure Cook or Manual, and adjust the pressure to High and the time to 3 minutes. Make sure the steam release knob is in the sealed position. After cooking, naturally release the pressure for 3 minutes, then quick release any remaining pressure. Unlock and remove the lid. Let the rice cool for 15 minutes. Using a fork, fluff the rice. Serve hot.

VEGETABLE BIRYANI

GLUTEN-FREE, NUT-FREE

SERVES 6

PREP AND FINISHING: 10 MINUTES, PLUS 15 MINUTES TO COOL

SAUTÉ: 10 MINUTES

PRESSURE COOK:
4 MINUTES ON HIGH

RELEASE: NATURAL
3 MINUTES, THEN QUICK

TOTAL TIME: 50 MINUTES

INGREDIENT TIP: YOU CAN BUY ANY BAG OF MIXED VEGETABLES. I LIKE CARROTS, CAULIFLOWER, GREEN BEANS, FROZEN PEAS, POTATO, AND CORN.

Per Serving
Calories: 240; Fat: 5g;
Carbohydrates: 45g;
Fiber: 2g; Protein: 5g;
Sodium: 489mg

Biryani is another staple in Indian cooking. For me, making this flavorful and fragrant rice dish is a standard weekend ritual. The whole spices and fresh mint leaves add an abundance of fragrant flavor. There are different varieties of biryani from the Indian subcontinent. Here is my easy, delicious vegetarian version.

2 tablespoons butter

3 cardamom seeds

3 whole cloves

2 dried bay leaves

1 (2-inch) cinnamon stick

1 onion, finely chopped

2 garlic cloves, finely chopped

2 teaspoons finely chopped fresh ginger

1½ cups roughly chopped fresh mint leaves

2 tomatoes, finely chopped

1½ teaspoons kosher salt

2 teaspoons ground coriander

1 teaspoon red chili powder

2 tablespoons plain Greek yogurt, plus more for serving

2 cups mixed vegetables

4 tablespoons finely chopped fresh cilantro, divided

1½ cups basmati rice

2¼ cups water

1. Make the biryani masala. Select Sauté, and melt the butter. Add the cardamom, cloves, bay leaves, and cinnamon stick. Fry for 30 seconds, then add the onion, garlic, ginger, and mint leaves. Sauté for 3 to 4 minutes or until the onion is translucent. Add the tomatoes and salt. Loosely place the lid on top, and cook for 3 minutes or until the tomatoes are soft. Add the coriander, chili powder, and yogurt. Mix well, and cook for 2 more minutes. Add the mixed vegetables and 2 tablespoons of cilantro, and mix well. Stir in the rice and water.

2. Pressure cook the rice. Lock the lid into place. Select Pressure Cook or Manual, and adjust the pressure to High and the time to 4 minutes. Make sure the steam release knob is in the sealed position. After cooking, naturally release the pressure for 3 minutes, then quick release any remaining pressure.

3. Finish the rice. Unlock and remove the lid. Let the rice cool for 15 minutes, and remove the bay leaves. Using a fork, fluff the rice and stir in the remaining 2 tablespoons of cilantro. Serve hot with additional yogurt.

VEGETABLE JAMBALAYA

NUT-FREE

SERVES 8

PREP AND FINISHING: 10 MINUTES,
PLUS 15 MINUTES TO COOL

SAUTÉ: 10 MINUTES

PRESSURE COOK:
12 MINUTES ON LOW

RELEASE: NATURAL

TOTAL TIME: 55 MINUTES

GLUTEN-FREE: USE TAMARI
SAUCE IN PLACE OF THE SOY
SAUCE (MAKE SURE THE
LABEL SAYS GLUTEN-FREE).

Per Serving
Calories: 262; Fat: 7g;
Carbohydrates: 41g;
Fiber: 4g; Protein: 10g;
Sodium: 873mg

Rice is my family's carbohydrate staple. I tend to gravitate toward easy, one-pot dishes that are loaded with vegetables and have rice as the base. This vegetarian jambalaya is one recipe that fits the bill. By adding the beans, I've boosted the protein intake and made the dish a complete meal on its own.

2 tablespoons corn oil

1 dried bay leaf

1 onion, finely chopped

2 garlic cloves, finely chopped

1 green serrano chile, finely chopped

4 tomatoes, finely chopped

½ teaspoon cayenne pepper

½ teaspoon paprika

½ teaspoon dried thyme

1 teaspoon dried oregano

1½ teaspoons kosher salt

½ teaspoon sugar

2 teaspoons soy sauce

1 cup chopped bell pepper

1 cup halved mushrooms

3 celery stalks, cut into 1-inch pieces

1 medium carrot, cut into 1-inch pieces

1 cup cooked black beans

4 tablespoons finely chopped fresh cilantro, divided

1½ cups short grain white rice

3 cups vegetable broth

½ cup shredded Mexican-blend cheese

1. **Sauté the tomatoes.** Select Sauté, and pour in the oil. Once hot, add the bay leaf, onion, garlic, and chile. Sauté for 3 to 4 minutes or until the onion is translucent. Add the tomatoes, cayenne pepper, paprika, thyme, oregano, salt, and sugar, and stir well. Loosely place the lid on top, and cook for 3 minutes or until the tomatoes are soft.

2. **Sauté the vegetables.** Add the soy sauce, then the bell pepper, mushrooms, celery, carrot, beans, and 2 tablespoons of cilantro. Mix in the rice and broth.

3. **Pressure cook the rice.** Lock the lid into place. Select Rice. Make sure the steam release knob is in the sealed position. After cooking, naturally release the pressure.

4. **Finish the jambalaya.** Unlock and remove the lid. Let the rice cool for 15 minutes, then remove the bay leaf. Using a fork, gently fluff the rice. Stir in the cheese and the remaining 2 tablespoons of cilantro, and serve hot.

MAC 'N CHEESE WITH SWEET POTATO SAUCE

NUT-FREE

SERVES 6

PREP AND FINISHING: 10 MINUTES, PLUS 15 MINUTES TO COOL

SAUTÉ: 5 + 5 MINUTES

PRESSURE COOK: 10 + 3 MINUTES ON HIGH

RELEASE: NATURAL + QUICK

SAUTÉ: 15 MINUTES

TOTAL TIME: 1 HOUR 25 MINUTES

MAKE IT VEGAN: INSTEAD OF CREAM, USE ALMOND MILK, AND SKIP THE CHEESE.

Per Serving
Calories: 561; Fat: 20g; Carbohydrates: 83g; Fiber: 7g; Protein: 17g; Sodium: 787mg

I love to make different pasta sauces with vegetables. This creamy sweet potato sauce is my kiddo's favorite. You can make the sweet potato sauce in batches over the weekend, then just cook the pasta and toss it with the sauce when you're ready to eat. You'll have dinner in under 15 minutes—I call that a win.

2 tablespoons extra-virgin olive oil, divided

1 cup roughly chopped onion

5 cups (1-inch pieces) peeled and cubed sweet potatoes

2 teaspoons kosher salt, divided

½ tablespoon freshly ground black pepper

7 cups water, divided

1 pound cavatappi pasta

½ cup heavy (whipping) cream

1 cup shredded mild Cheddar cheese

1 teaspoon dried basil

1. **Prepare the sweet potato sauce.** Select Sauté, and pour in 1½ tablespoons of oil. Once hot, add the onion and cook until it is translucent, about 5 minutes. Stir in the sweet potatoes, 1 teaspoon of salt, pepper, and 2 cups of water.

2. **Pressure cook the sauce.** Lock the lid into place. Select Pressure Cook or Manual, and adjust the pressure to High and the time to 10 minutes. Make sure the steam release knob is in the sealed position. After cooking, naturally release the pressure.

3. **Finish the sauce.** Unlock and remove the lid. Let the sweet potatoes cool for 15 minutes. Using an immersion blender, purée the sweet potato mixture. Transfer the sweet potato purée to a container. Clean the Instant Pot®.

4. Pressure cook the pasta. Pour the remaining 5 cups of water into the inner pot, and add the pasta. Add the remaining 1 teaspoon of salt and ½ tablespoon of oil, and stir gently. Lock the lid into place. Select Pressure Cook or Manual, and adjust the pressure to High and the time to 3 minutes. After cooking, quick release the pressure.

5. Assemble the mac 'n cheese. Unlock and remove the lid. Drain the pasta. Wipe out the pot. Select Sauté, and add the pasta, cream, and sweet potato sauce. Mix thoroughly, and let simmer for 3 minutes. Stir in the cheese, and cook until the cheese is melted, 1 to 2 minutes. Top with the basil, and serve hot.

PASTA PRIMAVERA

NUT-FREE

SERVES 6

PREP AND FINISHING: 10 MINUTES

PRESSURE COOK:
4 MINUTES ON HIGH

RELEASE: QUICK

SAUTÉ: 7 MINUTES

TOTAL TIME: 30 MINUTES

PAIR IT: PAIR THIS DISH WITH
TOMATO-BASIL SOUP (PAGE 58)
FOR A FRESH AND FILLING MEAL.

Per Serving
Calories: 315; Fat: 11g;
Carbohydrates: 47g;
Fiber: 3g; Protein: 11g;
Sodium: 1,029mg

It's believed that Pasta Primavera first debuted in New York City in the 1980s at one of the city's landmark restaurants, Le Cirque. While the restaurant is no longer around, their signature dish carries on. Pasta Primavera is truly a year-round dish. You can use any seasonal vegetables in the recipe—that's why it's in heavy rotation at my house. The fresh basil and lemon zest really boost the flavors of the fresh vegetables.

FOR THE PASTA

5 cups water

1 pound penne pasta

1 teaspoon extra-virgin olive oil

2 teaspoons kosher salt

FOR THE VEGETABLES

2 tablespoons extra-virgin olive oil

1 tablespoon butter

1 cup (1-inch pieces) chopped asparagus

1 cup (1-inch pieces) chopped carrots

1 zucchini, cut into bite-size pieces

1 teaspoon Italian dried herb seasoning

2 tablespoons finely chopped fresh basil leaves

1 teaspoon kosher salt

1 teaspoon freshly ground black pepper

1 teaspoon grated lemon zest

½ cup grated Parmesan cheese

1. **Pressure cook the pasta.** Pour the water into the inner pot, and add the pasta. Stir in the oil and salt. Lock the lid into place. Select Pressure Cook or Manual, and adjust the pressure to High and the time to 4 minutes. Make sure the steam release knob is in the sealed position. After cooking, quick release the pressure. Unlock and remove the lid. Drain the pasta, reserving about 2 tablespoons of pasta water.

2. **Assemble the pasta primavera.** Select Sauté, pour in the olive oil, and add the butter. Once hot, add the asparagus, carrot, zucchini, Italian seasoning, basil, salt, and pepper. Add the reserved pasta water, and mix well. Cook for 7 minutes or until the vegetables are tender. Stir in the pasta, lemon zest, and cheese, and serve hot.

SPAGHETTI "NOT" BOLOGNESE

NUT-FREE

SERVES 6

PREP AND FINISHING: 10 MINUTES

PRESSURE COOK: 2 +
5 MINUTES ON HIGH

RELEASE: NATURAL 5 MINUTES,
THEN QUICK + NATURAL

SAUTÉ: 3 MINUTES

TOTAL TIME: 35 MINUTES

MAKE IT VEGAN: SKIP THE
CHEESE OR USE VEGAN
PARMESAN CHEESE.

Per Serving
Calories: 396; Fat: 7g;
Carbohydrates: 66g;
Fiber: 11g; Protein: 20g;
Sodium: 984mg

Here is my vegetarian take on spaghetti Bolognese, made with mushrooms and lentils. The lentils add a unique texture to the sauce, while the mushrooms bring an earthiness to the dish. This Bolognese sauce is great to make in advance. It stores well in the refrigerator and freezer, so when you're having one of those busy weeknights, just reheat it and toss it with any pasta. Another dinner in minutes!

FOR THE PASTA

5 cups water

8 ounces spaghetti pasta

1 teaspoon extra-virgin olive oil

1 teaspoon kosher salt

FOR THE SAUCE

1 tablespoon extra-virgin olive oil

1 onion, finely chopped

5 garlic cloves, finely chopped

2 cups canned crushed tomatoes

¼ cup finely chopped fresh basil leaves

½ cup dried green lentils

5 baby bella mushrooms, roughly chopped

1 teaspoon kosher salt

2 teaspoons freshly ground black pepper

1 cup vegetable broth

½ cup shredded Parmesan cheese

1. **Pressure cook the pasta.** Pour the water into the inner pot, and add the spaghetti, olive oil, and salt. Stir gently. Lock the lid into place. Select Pressure Cook or Manual, and adjust the pressure to High and the time to 2 minutes. Make sure the steam release knob is in the sealed position. After cooking, naturally release the pressure for 5 minutes, then quick release any remaining pressure. Unlock and remove the lid. Drain the pasta.

2. **Prepare the sauce.** Select Sauté, and pour in the oil. Once hot, add the onion and garlic and cook until the onion is translucent, about 3 minutes. Stir in the tomatoes, basil, lentils, mushrooms, salt, pepper, and broth. Mix thoroughly.

→

3. Pressure cook the sauce. Lock the lid into place. Select Pressure Cook or Manual, and adjust the pressure to High and the time to 5 minutes. Make sure the steam release knob is in the sealed position. After cooking, naturally release the pressure.

4. Assemble the spaghetti Bolognese. Unlock and remove the lid. Using a potato masher, mash the lentils and tomatoes to get a chunky texture. Stir in the spaghetti, sprinkle with the cheese, and serve hot.

MUSHROOM STROGANOFF

NUT-FREE

SERVES 4

PREP AND FINISHING:
10 MINUTES, PLUS AT LEAST
5 MINUTES TO REST

PRESSURE COOK:
3 MINUTES ON HIGH

RELEASE: QUICK

SAUTÉ: 13 MINUTES

TOTAL TIME: 40 MINUTES

MAKE IT NEW: CUT YOUR CARBS BY SKIPPING THE PASTA. ADD 1/2 CUP MORE BROTH TO TURN THIS INTO CREAM OF MUSHROOM SOUP.

Per Serving
Calories: 425; Fat: 16g;
Carbohydrates: 62g;
Fiber: 5g; Protein: 13g;
Sodium: 903mg

Traditional stroganoff is made with tender strips of beef. My version replaces the meat with hearty baby bella mushrooms. These mushrooms really lend themselves to the rich and creamy sauce that stroganoff is known and loved for. I ladle this stroganoff over fusilli pasta, but use whichever type you like.

3 cups fusilli pasta

4 cups water

2 teaspoons kosher salt, divided

1 tablespoon plus 1 teaspoon corn oil, divided

2 tablespoons butter

1 yellow onion, roughly chopped

4 scallions, white parts only, finely chopped

2 garlic cloves, finely chopped

1 pound baby bella mushrooms, halved

1 teaspoon freshly ground black pepper

1 cup vegetable stock

2 tablespoons all-purpose flour

2 teaspoons Dijon mustard

1/3 cup sour cream

1/2 teaspoon sugar

1. Pressure cook the pasta. Add the pasta and water to the inner pot. Stir in 1/2 teaspoon of salt and 1 teaspoon of oil. Lock the lid into place. Select Pressure Cook or Manual, and adjust the pressure to High and the time to 3 minutes. Make sure the steam release knob is in the sealed position. After cooking, quick release the pressure. Unlock and remove the lid. Drain the pasta, reserving and setting aside about 4 tablespoons of pasta water.

→

2. Prepare the sauce. Select Sauté, and add the butter and remaining 1 tablespoon of oil. Once hot, add the onion, scallions, and garlic. Sauté for about 3 minutes. Add the mushrooms. Season with the pepper and the remaining 1½ teaspoons of salt, and cook until the mushrooms are soft and tender, about 5 minutes. Stir them only twice during this time. Add the stock. Deglaze the bottom of the pan, stirring to scrape up the browned bits from the bottom, and mix the ingredients thoroughly. Simmer for 2 minutes. In a small bowl, mix together the flour and the reserved pasta water until smooth. Add the slurry and the mustard to the sauce and mix thoroughly, ensuring there aren't any lumps. Thicken the sauce for about 3 minutes. Select Keep Warm.

3. Finish the sauce. Stir in the sour cream and sugar until well incorporated. Cover with the lid and let the sauce rest for at least 5 minutes. Serve over the pasta.

BARLEY-MUSHROOM "RISOTTO"

NUT-FREE

SERVES 6

PREP AND FINISHING: 10 MINUTES

SAUTÉ: 9 MINUTES

PRESSURE COOK:
30 MINUTES ON HIGH

RELEASE: NATURAL

TOTAL TIME: 1 HOUR

INGREDIENT TIP: USING DIFFERENT VARIETIES OF MUSHROOM ADDS DEPTH OF FLAVOR TO THE RISOTTO. YOU CAN ALSO USE JUST ONE VARIETY OR OPT FOR DRIED MUSHROOMS. IF USING DRIED, SOAK THEM IN HOT WATER FOR AT LEAST 30 MINUTES, THEN ADD THE MUSHROOMS ALONG WITH THEIR SOAKING WATER TO THE INSTANT POT®. OVERALL COOK TIME AND PRESSURE REMAIN THE SAME.

Per Serving
Calories: 257; Fat: 9g;
Carbohydrates: 33g;
Fiber: 6g; Protein: 12g;
Sodium: 913mg

Risotto is a rich rice dish that is popular in Italy. Traditional risottos use Arborio rice and require a lot of time and constant stirring over the stove. My version calls for barley, and the Instant Pot® does all the work. With the flavors of different mushrooms, cheese, and barley, this "risotto" is definitely a feast.

3 tablespoons butter

1 onion, finely chopped

1 cup coarsely chopped cremini mushrooms

1 cup coarsely chopped shiitake mushrooms

1 cup coarsely chopped brown bella mushrooms

1 teaspoon kosher salt

1 teaspoon freshly ground black pepper

1 teaspoon Italian dried herb seasoning

1 cup pearl barley

1 (32-ounce) container vegetable broth

½ cup shredded Parmesan cheese

1. **Sauté the vegetables.** Select Sauté, and melt the butter. Add the onion, and cook until the onion is translucent, about 3 minutes. Mix in the mushrooms, salt, pepper, and Italian seasoning. Cook for 5 to 6 minutes or until the mushrooms shrink. Stir in the barley and broth.

2. **Pressure cook the barley.** Lock the lid into place. Select Pressure Cook or Manual, and adjust the pressure to High and the time to 30 minutes. Make sure the steam release knob is in the sealed position. After cooking, naturally release the pressure. Unlock and remove the lid. Stir in the Parmesan cheese. Mix well and serve hot.

UDON NOODLES IN PEANUT SAUCE

DAIRY-FREE, VEGAN

SERVES 4

PREP AND FINISHING: 10 MINUTES

PRESSURE COOK:
3 MINUTES ON HIGH

RELEASE: QUICK

SAUTÉ: 4 MINUTES

TOTAL TIME: 25 MINUTES

TRY THIS: INSTEAD OF PEANUT BUTTER, USE ANY NUT BUTTER OF YOUR CHOICE. FOR A MILDER NUTTY FLAVOR, I RECOMMEND UNSWEETENED ALMOND BUTTER.

Per Serving
Calories: 180; Fat: 8g;
Carbohydrates: 23g;
Fiber: 3g; Protein: 6g;
Sodium: 721mg

Udon noodles are extremely popular in Japan. Made from wheat flour, the sturdy noodle can be served cold in a salad, hot in a soup, or mixed with a sauce as in this recipe. The sweetness of peanut butter and the heat from Sriracha make for an interesting blend and balance of flavors. Best of all? It's super easy to make on busy weeknights.

4 ounces or 2 individually wrapped bundles udon noodles

4 cups water

½ teaspoon kosher salt, divided

1 teaspoon corn oil

1 tablespoon peanut oil

6 scallions, white parts only, finely chopped

1 teaspoon finely chopped fresh ginger

1 garlic clove, finely chopped

2 teaspoons soy sauce

1 teaspoon Sriracha

1 tablespoon peanut butter

1 teaspoon white sesame seeds

1. Pressure cook the noodles. Put the noodles in the inner pot with enough water to fully cover the noodles. Gently stir in ¼ teaspoon of salt and the corn oil. Lock the lid into place. Select Pressure Cook or Manual, and adjust the pressure to High and the time to 3 minutes. Make sure the steam release knob is in the sealed position. After cooking, quick release the pressure. Unlock and remove the lid. Drain the noodles, and run cold water over them. Set aside.

2. Prepare the peanut sauce. Select Sauté, and pour in the peanut oil. Once hot, add the scallions, ginger, and garlic, and sauté for 2 minutes. Add the soy sauce, Sriracha, peanut butter, and remaining ¼ teaspoon of salt. Mix until the peanut butter has thinned and combined with the other ingredients. Add the noodles, and gently stir for 1 minute. Serve hot, sprinkled with the sesame seeds.

VEGETABLE LO MEIN

DAIRY-FREE, VEGAN

SERVES 4

PREP AND FINISHING: 10 MINUTES

PRESSURE COOK:
2 MINUTES ON HIGH

RELEASE: QUICK

SAUTÉ: 3 MINUTES

TOTAL TIME: 20 MINUTES

TRY THIS: IF YOU DON'T HAVE LO MEIN NOODLES, TRY USING SOBA NOODLES OR EVEN WHOLE WHEAT PASTA. THERE'S NO NEED TO SOAK THESE NOODLES; JUST COOK ON HIGH FOR 2 MINUTES. YOU CAN ALSO COOK THE NOODLES AHEAD AND STORE THEM IN THE FRIDGE. IN THAT CASE, ADD 2 TEASPOONS OF OIL TO THE COOKED NOODLES BEFORE STORING TO KEEP THEM FROM STICKING TOGETHER.

Per Serving
Calories: 351; Fat: 9g;
Carbohydrates: 60g;
Fiber: 3g; Protein: 8g;
Sodium: 1,250mg

I make this dish at least once a week for my family. We love how the soft noodles absorb the sauce. Lo mein noodles cook really fast and can quickly become too soft, but using the Instant Pot® delivers just the right texture every time.

10 ounces (2 bundles) dried lo mein noodles

4 cups water

1 teaspoon kosher salt, divided

1 teaspoon corn oil

2 tablespoons peanut oil

5 scallions, white parts only, finely chopped

3 garlic cloves, finely chopped

¼ cup (1-inch pieces) chopped green beans

¼ cup thinly sliced red bell pepper

¼ cup shredded green cabbage

¼ cup (1-inch matchsticks) julienned carrots

1 teaspoon freshly ground black pepper

2 tablespoons soy sauce

1 tablespoon teriyaki sauce

1 tablespoon Sriracha

1 tablespoon maple syrup

1. Soak the noodles. In a medium bowl, soak the noodles in water for 5 minutes, then drain.

2. Pressure cook the noodles. Pour the water into the inner pot, then add the noodles, ½ teaspoon of salt, and the corn oil, stirring gently. Lock the lid into place. Select Pressure Cook or Manual, and adjust the pressure to High and the time to 2 minutes. Make sure the steam release knob is in the sealed position. After cooking, quick release the pressure. Drain the noodles, then run them under cold water to stop the cooking. Set aside.

3. Prepare the vegetables. Select Sauté, adjust the heat to More, and add the peanut oil. Once hot, add the scallions, garlic, green beans, bell pepper, cabbage, carrot, the remaining ½ teaspoon of salt, and pepper. Cook for 3 minutes, stirring constantly. Stir in the soy sauce, teriyaki sauce, Sriracha, and maple syrup. Add the noodles, and gently mix. Serve hot.

*Apple-Cinnamon
Oat Porridge*

PAGE 98

Chapter Six
OTHER GRAINS

APPLE-CINNAMON OAT PORRIDGE

GLUTEN-FREE

SERVES 4

PREP AND FINISHING: 10 MINUTES

PRESSURE COOK:
5 MINUTES ON HIGH

RELEASE: NATURAL
10 MINUTES, THEN QUICK

TOTAL TIME: 35 MINUTES

MAKE IT VEGAN: REPLACE
THE MILK WITH ALMOND MILK,
SOY MILK, OR YOUR FAVORITE
PLANT-BASED MILK.

Per Serving
Calories: 216; Fat: 8g;
Carbohydrates: 33g;
Fiber: 4g; Protein: 6g;
Sodium: 47mg

Instant Pot® oatmeal is one of my all-time favorite things to make. For starters it's super easy, and my recipe is set up so you can make a big batch over the weekend and have it available all week long. My family's favorite is oatmeal with apples and cinnamon, but feel free to add your own favorite fruits and spices.

1½ cups old-fashioned rolled oats

1½ cups milk

3½ cups water, divided

1 (½-inch) cinnamon stick

4 tablespoons brown sugar

2 apples, finely chopped, divided

1 teaspoon ground cinnamon

¼ cup roughly chopped walnuts

1. **Pressure cook the oats.** In a small bowl that fits inside your Instant Pot®, mix together the oats, milk, 2 cups of water, and cinnamon stick. Pour the remaining 1½ cups of water into the inner pot, and place the trivet inside. Place the bowl on the trivet, and lock the lid into place. Select Pressure Cook or Manual, and adjust the pressure to High and the time to 5 minutes. Make sure the steam release knob is in the sealed position. After cooking, naturally release the pressure for 10 minutes, then quick release any remaining pressure.

2. **Assemble the oatmeal.** Unlock and remove the lid. Remove the bowl, and mix the oats thoroughly. Stir in the sugar, 1 chopped apple, ground cinnamon, and walnuts. Top with the remaining 1 chopped apple and serve warm.

SAVORY RICE PORRIDGE

DAIRY-FREE, NUT-FREE, VEGAN

SERVES 8

PREP AND FINISHING: 10 MINUTES

SAUTÉ: 4 MINUTES

PRESSURE COOK:
20 MINUTES ON HIGH

RELEASE: NATURAL

TOTAL TIME: 45 MINUTES

MAKE IT GLUTEN-FREE: USE
TAMARI SAUCE IN PLACE OF THE
SOY SAUCE (MAKE SURE THE
LABEL SAYS GLUTEN-FREE).

Per Serving
Calories: 107; Fat: 2g;
Carbohydrates: 20g;
Fiber: 1g; Protein: 2g;
Sodium: 628mg

Congee is a popular rice porridge in many Asian countries. Savory in nature, it can be served as a side dish. However, if you add other ingredients to it, the porridge becomes a meal in and of itself. I love congee for breakfast. Here's my take on a savory congee with a hint of soy sauce and mushrooms.

1 tablespoon sesame oil

½ cup finely chopped scallions, white and green parts, divided

1 cup halved white mushrooms

1 teaspoon kosher salt

1 teaspoon freshly ground black pepper

9 teaspoons soy sauce, divided

1 cup sticky rice, rinsed

5 cups water

1. **Sauté the mushrooms.** Select Sauté, and pour in the oil. Once hot, add ¼ cup of scallions and the mushrooms, salt, and pepper. Sauté for 3 to 4 minutes or until the mushrooms start to brown. Stir in 1 teaspoon of soy sauce, then stir in the rice and water.

2. **Pressure cook the porridge.** Lock the lid into place. Select Porridge. Make sure the steam release knob is in the sealed position. After cooking, naturally release the pressure.

3. **Assemble the Congee.** Unlock and remove the lid. Using a potato masher or the back of a ladle, mash the rice until mushy. Stir in the remaining ¼ cup of scallions and 8 teaspoons of soy sauce, and serve hot.

COUSCOUS PILAF

NUT-FREE

SERVES 4

PREP AND FINISHING: 5 MINUTES, PLUS 10 MINUTES TO COOL

SAUTÉ: 7 MINUTES

PRESSURE COOK: 3 MINUTES ON HIGH

RELEASE: NATURAL 5 MINUTES, THEN QUICK

TOTAL TIME: 35 MINUTES

MAKE IT VEGAN: REPLACE THE BUTTER WITH COCONUT OIL OR EXTRA-VIRGIN OLIVE OIL.

Per Serving
Calories: 279; Fat: 21g; Carbohydrates: 21g; Fiber: 3g; Protein: 5g; Sodium: 491mg

Pilaf, a rich dish cooked with vegetables and spices, is quite popular in the Middle East and Asia. Traditionally, it is prepared with rice, but I love to make a pilaf with other grains as well. My take here uses pearl couscous cooked in coconut milk, which makes the dish rich and creamy.

1 tablespoon butter

1 dried bay leaf

3 cardamom seeds

3 whole cloves

1 (1-inch) cinnamon stick

1 onion, thinly sliced

1 green Thai chile, split lengthwise

¼ cup frozen peas, thawed to room temperature

¼ cup frozen corn, thawed to room temperature

1 cup pearl couscous, rinsed and drained

1 cup full-fat coconut milk

1 teaspoon kosher salt

1. **Sauté the spices and onion.** Select Sauté, and melt the butter. Add the bay leaf, cardamom, cloves, and cinnamon stick, and sauté for 30 seconds. Add the onions and chile, and cook for 4 to 5 minutes or until the onion is translucent. Add the peas and corn, and cook for another minute. Stir in the couscous, coconut milk, and salt until well combined.

2. **Pressure cook the couscous.** Lock the lid into place. Select Pressure Cook or Manual, and adjust the pressure to High and the time to 3 minutes. Make sure the steam release knob is in the sealed position. After cooking, naturally release the pressure for 5 minutes, then quick release any remaining pressure. Unlock and remove the lid. Let the couscous cool for 10 minutes, then remove the bay leaf. Fluff the couscous with a fork, and serve hot.

COUSCOUS SALAD WITH CUCUMBER, OLIVES, AND CARROT

DAIRY-FREE, NUT-FREE, VEGAN

SERVES 6

PREP AND FINISHING: 20 MINUTES

PRESSURE COOK:
2 MINUTES ON HIGH

RELEASE: NATURAL
5 MINUTES, THEN QUICK

TOTAL TIME: 35 MINUTES

INGREDIENT TIP: TRY THIS WITH PEARL COUSCOUS, ALSO KNOWN AS ISRAELI COUSCOUS, OR EVEN BULGUR WHEAT. FOR PEARL COUSCOUS, INCREASE THE COOK TIME BY 1 MINUTE. FOR BULGUR WHEAT, THE COOK TIME REMAINS THE SAME.

Per Serving
Calories: 164; Fat: 6g;
Carbohydrates: 25g;
Fiber: 2g; Protein: 4g;
Sodium: 359mg

I love to fill my plate with color, especially when I make salads. This couscous recipe is loaded with bright red, orange, green, and purple vegetables—a veritable rainbow of natural goodness. Two of the vegetables are marinated before you toss them into the salad, adding a layer of bold flavor.

FOR THE COUSCOUS

1 cup couscous

2¾ cups water, divided

FOR THE SALAD

½ cup salad greens (such as a mix of spinach, arugula, and red and green lettuce leaves)

4 tablespoons finely chopped carrot

4 tablespoons finely chopped black olives

4 tablespoons finely chopped cucumber

½ cup thinly sliced red onion, marinated in 2 tablespoons each of lemon juice and water for 20 minutes, then drained

½ cup shredded red cabbage, marinated in 2 tablespoons each of lemon juice and water for 20 minutes, then drained

1 teaspoon kosher salt

1 teaspoon freshly ground black pepper

2 tablespoons extra-virgin olive oil

1. Pressure cook the couscous. Put the couscous and 1¼ cups of water in a heatproof bowl that fits inside the Instant Pot®. Add the remaining 1½ cups of water to the inner pot, and place the trivet inside. Place the bowl on the trivet. Lock the lid into place. Select Pressure Cook or Manual, and adjust the pressure to High and the time to 2 minutes. Make sure the steam release knob is in the sealed position. After cooking, naturally release the pressure for 5 minutes, then quick release any remaining pressure. Unlock and remove the lid. Let the couscous cool for 15 minutes before fluffing with a fork.

2. Assemble the salad. Add the salad greens, carrot, olives, cucumber, onion, cabbage, salt, pepper, and olive oil to the couscous. Mix gently and serve.

FARRO AND SPINACH SALAD

NUT-FREE

SERVES 4

PREP AND FINISHING: 10 MINUTES

PRESSURE COOK:
3 MINUTES ON HIGH

RELEASE: NATURAL
5 MINUTES, THEN QUICK

SAUTÉ: 7 MINUTES

TOTAL TIME: 35 MINUTES

MAKE IT VEGAN: REPLACE THE
BUTTER WITH EXTRA-VIRGIN
OLIVE OIL OR CORN OIL.

Per Serving
Calories: 87; Fat: 6g;
Carbohydrates: 8g;
Fiber: 1g; Protein: 2g;
Sodium: 518mg

I love to combine grains and vegetables for a simple but super healthy stir-fry. This salad is one of my go-to midday meals. I often turn to it for a quick and easy side dish at dinner. I like the combination of nutty farro and sweet, earthy spinach. Plus, it also packs a one-two punch of fiber and iron—what more could you want?

FOR THE FARRO

½ cup farro

1 cup water

FOR THE SPINACH

2 tablespoons butter

4 garlic cloves, finely chopped

4 cups baby spinach, roughly chopped

1 teaspoon red chili flakes

1 teaspoon kosher salt

1. Pressure cook the farro. Pour the water into the inner pot, and add the farro. Lock the lid into place. Select Pressure Cook or Manual, and adjust the pressure to High and the time to 3 minutes. Make sure the steam release knob is in the sealed position. After cooking, naturally release the pressure for 5 minutes, then quick release any remaining pressure. Unlock and remove the lid. Drain the farro.

2. Sauté the spinach. Select Sauté, and melt the butter. Add the garlic, and sauté for 30 seconds. Add the spinach, red chili flakes, and salt. Cook until the spinach wilts, about 5 minutes. Add the farro, and sauté for 1 minute. Serve hot.

POLENTA WITH MUSHROOMS

GLUTEN-FREE, NUT-FREE

SERVES 4

PREP AND FINISHING: 5 MINUTES

SAUTÉ: 3 MINUTES

PRESSURE COOK:
20 MINUTES ON HIGH

RELEASE: NATURAL

TOTAL TIME: 40 MINUTES

MAKE IT VEGAN: REPLACE
THE BUTTER WITH EXTRA-
VIRGIN OLIVE OIL.

Per Serving
Calories: 183; Fat: 5g;
Carbohydrates: 26g;
Fiber: 2g; Protein: 8g;
Sodium: 1367mg

I love all types of polenta: creamy, semi-soft, and hard-cooked. But, the stove top method of cooking it is time consuming and labor intensive because you have to constantly stir it. With an Instant Pot®, you can make delicious, lump-free polenta, no stirring required. Cooking the mushrooms along with the polenta brings an earthiness to the dish that I think you'll find delectable.

1 cup yellow cornmeal

4 cups vegetable broth

1 tablespoon butter

2 portobello mushrooms caps, finely chopped

1 teaspoon onion powder

1 teaspoon kosher salt

1 teaspoon freshly ground black pepper

1. Prepare the cornmeal mix. In a large bowl, whisk together the cornmeal and broth until there are no lumps. Set aside.

2. Sauté the mushrooms. Select Sauté, and melt the butter. Add the mushrooms, onion powder, salt, and pepper, and sauté for 2 minutes. Add the cornmeal mix to the pot. Mix well, making sure to scrape the bottom of the pot.

3. Pressure cook the polenta. Lock the lid into place. Select Porridge. Make sure the steam release knob is in the sealed position. After cooking, naturally release the pressure. Unlock and remove the lid. Stir the polenta a few turns, and serve hot.

SWEET CORN TAMALITO

GLUTEN-FREE, NUT-FREE

SERVES 4

PREP AND FINISHING: 10 MINUTES

PRESSURE COOK:
30 MINUTES ON HIGH

RELEASE: NATURAL

TOTAL TIME: 50 MINUTES

DOUBLE IT: YOU CAN DOUBLE
THE INGREDIENTS, BUT THE
COOK TIME WILL REMAIN THE
SAME. FOR A LARGE BATCH,
USE A SPRINGFORM PAN.

Per Serving
Calories: 175; Fat: 12g;
Carbohydrates: 17g; Fiber: 1g;
Protein: 2g; Sodium: 61mg

This rich and creamy sweet corn tamalito will surely satisfy your taste buds and sweet tooth. They are very easy to make, too. Also known as sweet corn masa cake, my version uses brown sugar instead of refined white sugar. The brown sugar keeps them from being too sweet, while adding depth of flavor.

¼ cup masa harina

½ cup frozen corn kernels, thawed to room temperature

3 tablespoons brown sugar

½ teaspoon baking powder

2 tablespoons butter, melted, plus 2 teaspoons butter, at room temperature

3 tablespoons heavy (whipping) cream

1 cup water

1. **Prepare the tamalito mix.** In a blender, combine the masa harina, corn, sugar, baking powder, melted butter, and cream. Pulse until the mixture looks coarse. Use the room-temperature butter to grease a heatproof bowl that will fit in the Instant Pot®. Transfer the tamalito mix to the bowl, and cover tightly with aluminum foil.

2. **Pressure cook the tamalito.** Pour the water into the inner pot, and place the trivet inside. Place the bowl on the trivet. Lock the lid into place. Select Pressure Cook or Manual, and adjust the pressure to High and the time to 30 minutes. Make sure the steam release knob is in the sealed position. After cooking, naturally release the pressure. Unlock and remove the lid. Remove the foil from the bowl. Cut the tamalito into 4 servings, and serve warm.

ENCHILADA CASSEROLE

NUT-FREE

SERVES 4

PREP AND FINISHING: 10 MINUTES,
PLUS 30 MINUTES TO COOL

PRESSURE COOK:
30 MINUTES ON HIGH

RELEASE: NATURAL

TOTAL TIME: 1 HOUR 20 MINUTES

MAKE IT GLUTEN-FREE:
INSTEAD OF FLOUR TORTILLAS,
YOU CAN USE CORN TORTILLAS.

Per Serving
Calories: 263; Fat: 11g;
Carbohydrates: 31g;
Fiber: 8g; Protein: 14g;
Sodium: 197mg

I love casseroles, especially those that require only two steps—assemble and bake. This enchilada casserole takes away all the time and effort of traditional enchiladas but still delivers the same satisfying flavor. It's a great recipe to serve at a potluck or for a busy weeknight dinner.

3 (6-inch) flour tortillas

4 tablespoons enchilada sauce, divided

2 zucchini, cut into rounds, divided

½ cup frozen corn kernels, thawed to room temperature, divided

½ cup chopped bell pepper, divided

1 cup canned black beans, rinsed and drained, divided

1 cup Mexican-blend shredded cheese, divided

1 cup water

1. **Assemble the casserole.** Place one tortilla in a spring-form pan. Spread 2 tablespoons of enchilada sauce on top. Layer half of the zucchini rounds on top of the sauce, then layer on ¼ cup each of corn and bell pepper and ½ cup of beans. Top with ½ cup of cheese. Repeat with the second tortilla and the remaining 2 tablespoons of sauce, ¼ cup each of corn and bell pepper, and ½ cup each of beans and cheese. Place the third tortilla on top. Tightly cover the pan with aluminum foil.

2. **Pressure cook the casserole.** Pour the water into the inner pot, and place the trivet inside. Place the springform pan on top of the trivet, and lock the lid into place. Select Pressure Cook or Manual, and adjust the pressure to High and the time to 30 minutes. Make sure the steam release knob is in the sealed position. After cooking, naturally release the pressure. Unlock and remove the lid. Remove the aluminum foil. Let cool for 30 minutes. Using a pizza cutter, cut the casserole into quarters. Serve warm.

ZA'ATAR-SPICED BULGUR WHEAT SALAD

DAIRY-FREE, NUT-FREE, VEGAN

SERVES 6

PREP AND FINISHING: 10 MINUTES,
PLUS 20 MINUTES TO COOL

PRESSURE COOK:
2 MINUTES ON HIGH

RELEASE: NATURAL
5 MINUTES, THEN QUICK

TOTAL TIME: 45 MINUTES

PAIR IT: THIS SALAD PAIRS REALLY
WELL WITH YELLOW SPLIT PEAS
WITH TURMERIC (PAGE 46).

Per Serving
Calories: 126; Fat: 5g;
Carbohydrates: 19g;
Fiber: 5g; Protein: 3g;
Sodium: 308mg

Fresh herbs always enhance the flavor of a dish. This bulgur wheat salad benefits from good amounts of parsley and mint. Both aromatic, they add a freshness to the dish that you can't find using dried herbs. The herbs also add lightness as a nice contrast to the hearty bulgur wheat.

FOR THE BULGUR WHEAT

1 cup bulgur wheat

2¼ cups water, divided

FOR THE SALAD

¼ cup finely chopped cucumber

¼ cup finely chopped fresh parsley

2 tablespoons finely chopped fresh mint

2 tablespoons extra-virgin olive oil

2 tablespoons freshly squeezed lemon juice

5 cherry tomatoes, finely chopped

1 teaspoon kosher salt

½ teaspoon freshly ground black pepper

1 teaspoon za'atar spice blend

1. **Pressure cook the bulgur wheat.** Put the bulgur wheat and 1¼ cups water in a heatproof bowl that fits inside the Instant Pot®. Pour 1 cup of water into the inner pot, and place the trivet inside. Place the bowl on the trivet. Lock the lid into place. Make sure the steam release knob is in the sealed position. Select Pressure Cook or Manual, and adjust the pressure to High and the time to 2 minutes. After cooking, naturally release the pressure for 5 minutes, then quick release any remaining pressure. Unlock and remove the lid. Let the bulgur wheat cool for 20 minutes, then fluff it with a fork.

2. **Assemble the salad.** Add the cucumber, parsley, mint, olive oil, lemon juice, tomatoes, salt, pepper, and za'atar seasoning to the bulgur wheat. Mix gently and serve.

Za'atar-Spiced
Bulgur Wheat Salad

Dulce de Leche

PAGE 118

Chapter Seven
DESSERTS

APPLE-PEAR CRISP

NUT-FREE

SERVES 4

PREP AND FINISHING: 10 MINUTES

PRESSURE COOK:
5 MINUTES ON HIGH

RELEASE: QUICK

SAUTÉ: 4 MINUTES

TOTAL TIME: 30 MINUTES

MAKE IT NEW: STIR THIS CRISP INTO YOUR OATMEAL FOR A DELICIOUS BREAKFAST.

Per Serving
Calories: 289; Fat: 9g;
Carbohydrates: 51g;
Fiber: 6g; Protein: 3g;
Sodium: 67mg

I love fruit-based desserts. They are a great way to sneak in servings of vitamins and minerals, plus they naturally enhance the flavors of the other ingredients. This crisp combines the goodness of whole oats with the natural sweetness of pears and apples. Be sure to serve it warm with vanilla ice cream for an extra dose of decadence.

3 tablespoons butter, melted

½ cup packed brown sugar

½ cup all-purpose flour

½ cup old-fashioned rolled oats

1 teaspoon ground cinnamon

½ teaspoon freshly grated nutmeg

2 gala apples, peeled, cored, and sliced (about 2½ cups)

2 Asian pears, peeled, cored, and sliced (about 2½ cups)

½ cup water

1. **Prepare the oat mixture.** In a small bowl, mix together the butter, brown sugar, flour, oats, cinnamon, and nutmeg.

2. **Assemble the crisp.** In the inner pot, evenly layer the apples and pears. Evenly spread the oat mixture on top of the fruit. Pour the water on top of the oat mixture.

3. **Pressure cook the crisp.** Lock the lid into place. Select Pressure Cook or Manual, and adjust the pressure to High and the time to 5 minutes. Make sure the steam release knob is in the sealed position. After cooking, quick release the pressure. Unlock and remove the lid. Select Sauté, and stir the crisp. Let it cook for 3 to 4 minutes, or until it bubbles, and serve warm.

STRAWBERRY-CHOCOLATE CAKE

NUT-FREE

SERVES 8

PREP AND FINISHING:
15 MINUTES, PLUS AT LEAST
30 MINUTES TO COOL

PRESSURE COOK:
30 MINUTES ON HIGH

RELEASE: NATURAL

TOTAL TIME: 1 HOUR 25 MINUTES

USE IT UP: THIS CAKE IS PERFECT
FOR MAKING CAKE POPS. CRUMBLE
THE LEFTOVER CAKE. STIR JUST
ENOUGH MELTED BUTTER INTO
THE CRUMBLES SO THEY HOLD
THEIR SHAPE WHEN FORMED
INTO BALLS. MAKE SMALL CAKE
BALLS, AND INSERT LOLLIPOP
STICKS INTO THE CAKE BALLS.

Per Serving
Calories: 448; Fat: 19g;
Carbohydrates: 66g; Fiber: 2g;
Protein: 4g; Sodium: 377mg

This is one of my family's favorite desserts and the cake I made for my son on his birthday. Strawberries and chocolate are a match made in heaven. Here, I purée the strawberries and add them directly to the cake batter. What you get is a rich and moist chocolate cake with the sweet and subtle flavor of strawberry laced throughout.

10 fresh strawberries, hulled, plus 10 fresh strawberries, hulled and halved

2 cups plus 1 tablespoon water, divided

1 cup sugar

½ cup plain Greek yogurt

½ teaspoon baking soda

1½ teaspoons baking powder

⅛ teaspoon kosher salt

1¼ cups all-purpose flour

2 tablespoons cocoa powder

½ cup corn oil

Nonstick cooking spray

1 cup vanilla cream cheese frosting

1. Prepare the strawberry purée. In a blender, combine the whole strawberries and 1 tablespoon of water. Purée until smooth. This should make about ½ cup of purée.

2. Prepare the yogurt mix. In a large bowl, whisk together the sugar and yogurt until the sugar is dissolved. Stir in the baking soda, baking powder, and salt. Let sit for about 5 minutes or until the mixture begins to bubble.

3. Sift the flour. Meanwhile, in a medium bowl, sift the flour and cocoa powder together.

4. Prepare the batter. Whisk the yogurt mixture again, then slowly whisk in the oil. Keep whisking until the oil is fully incorporated. Add the strawberry purée, and mix again. Add the flour-cocoa mixture, and gently mix to form a smooth batter.

➡

5. Bake the cake. Grease a springform pan with the cooking spray. Pour the batter into the pan, then tap the pan twice on the counter to break any air pockets. Tightly cover with aluminum foil. Pour the remaining 2 cups of water into the inner pot, and place the trivet inside. Place the pan on the trivet, and lock the lid into place. Select Pressure Cook or Manual, and adjust the pressure to High and the time to 30 minutes. Make sure the steam release knob is in the sealed position. After cooking, naturally release the pressure. Unlock and remove the lid. Remove the pan, and carefully remove the foil. Let cool for at least 30 minutes before removing the cake from the pan.

6. Decorate the cake. Evenly spread the frosting over the cake. Place the fresh strawberry halves on top and serve.

BREAD PUDDING

SERVES 6

PREP AND FINISHING: 10 MINUTES

PRESSURE COOK:
35 MINUTES ON HIGH

RELEASE: NATURAL

TOTAL TIME: 55 MINUTES

MAKE IT NUT-FREE: INSTEAD OF PECANS, ADD DRIED FRUIT SUCH AS APRICOTS OR FIGS.

Per Serving
Calories: 351; Fat: 26g;
Carbohydrates: 29g; Fiber: 1g;
Protein: 6g; Sodium: 227mg

My rich and creamy Bread Pudding is flavored with allspice, which brings a rich warmth to this dessert. It also doesn't contain eggs, unlike all the traditional recipes for this dessert. Instead, I use sweetened condensed milk to give the pudding that perfect amount of denseness.

1 cup heavy (whipping) cream

1 cup milk

½ cup sweetened condensed milk

2 tablespoons butter, melted, plus 1 tablespoon butter, at room temperature

1 teaspoon ground allspice

3 cups roughly chopped white bread

2 tablespoons raisins

10 pecans

2 cups water

1. Prepare the milk mixture. In a medium bowl, combine the cream, milk, and condensed milk. Add the melted butter and allspice, and mix thoroughly.

2. Assemble the bread pudding. Grease a springform pan with the room-temperature butter. Evenly layer the bread cubes in the pan. Pour the milk mixture on top, and let rest for 5 minutes so the bread soaks up the liquid. Sprinkle the raisins and pecans over the bread, and tightly cover the pan with aluminum foil.

3. Pressure cook the bread pudding. Pour the water into the inner pot, and place the trivet inside. Place the pan on top of the trivet, and lock the lid into place. Select Pressure Cook or Manual, and adjust the pressure to High and the time to 35 minutes. Make sure the steam release knob is in the sealed position. After cooking, naturally release the pressure. Unlock and remove the lid. Remove the pan, then carefully remove the foil. Let the pudding cool to the touch, then slice and serve it warm.

MANGO CHEESECAKE

NUT-FREE

SERVES 8

PREP AND FINISHING:
20 MINUTES, PLUS AT LEAST
7 HOURS TO COOL AND CHILL

PRESSURE COOK:
50 MINUTES ON HIGH

RELEASE: NATURAL

TOTAL TIME: 9 HOURS 20 MINUTES

INGREDIENT TIP: INSTEAD
OF MANGOS, YOU CAN USE
RASPBERRIES. MAKE SURE
TO STRAIN THE PURÉE TO
REMOVE THE SEEDS. INSTEAD
OF FRESH FRUIT, YOU CAN USE
FRUIT EXTRACTS. USE DULCE
DE LECHE (PAGE 118) FOR A
CARAMEL CHEESECAKE.

Per Serving
Calories: 484; Fat: 34g;
Carbohydrates: 43g; Fiber: 2g;
Protein: 6g; Sodium: 318mg

Mango is my favorite fruit. In my hometown in India, every meal usually includes at least one dish made with mango. This dessert is something I started to experiment with when I would get homesick for mango dishes. This cheesecake is destined to become one of your favorites, as it is mine.

1½ cups graham
cracker crumbs

½ cup unsalted butter, melted,
plus 1 tablespoon unsalted
butter, at room temperature

½ cup plus 2 tablespoons
sugar, divided

2 mangos, peeled and roughly
chopped, plus 1 mango, peeled
and thinly sliced

2 cups plus 2 tablespoons
water, divided

16 ounces cream cheese, at
room temperature

2 tablespoons cornstarch

1. **Prepare the crust.** In a medium bowl, mix together the graham cracker crumbs, melted butter, and 2 tablespoons of sugar. Reserve 2 tablespoons of the mixture to use as a garnish. Grease a springform pan with the room-temperature butter. Add the crumb mixture to the pan, and evenly press it down into the bottom. Place in the freezer for 15 minutes.

2. **Prepare the mango purée.** Meanwhile, in a blender, combine the 2 chopped mangos and 2 tablespoons of water. Purée until smooth. This should make about 1 cup.

3. Prepare the filling. In a large bowl, use a hand mixer to beat the cream cheese for 2 to 3 minutes or until light and fluffy. Add the remaining ½ cup of sugar, and mix until well combined. Add the cornstarch and mango purée. Using a spoon, gently fold the mixture until well combined. Remove the springform pan from the freezer, and pour the filling on top of the crust. Tightly cover the pan with aluminum foil.

4. Pressure cook the cheesecake. Pour the remaining 2 cups of water into the inner pot, and place the trivet inside. Place the pan on top of the trivet, and lock the lid into place. Select Pressure Cook or Manual, and adjust the pressure to High and the time to 50 minutes. Make sure the steam release knob is in the sealed position. After cooking, naturally release the pressure.

5. Finish the cheesecake. Unlock and remove the lid. Carefully remove the cake, then remove the foil. The center will be loose. Let it cool at room temperature for 1 hour, then cover the cheesecake again with foil and refrigerate for at least 6 hours. Before serving, sprinkle with the reserved crumb mixture and decorate with the sliced mangos.

CINNAMON YOGURT CUSTARD

GLUTEN-FREE, NUT-FREE

SERVES 4

PREP AND FINISHING:
10 MINUTES, PLUS 4 HOURS
TO COOL AND CHILL

PRESSURE COOK:
25 MINUTES ON HIGH

RELEASE: NATURAL

TOTAL TIME: 4 HOURS 45 MINUTES

INGREDIENT TIP: INSTEAD OF
CINNAMON, USE VANILLA, ALMOND,
OR ORANGE EXTRACT. YOU CAN
ALSO INCLUDE 1/4 TO 1/2 CUP OF
SWEET FRESH FRUIT PURÉE,
SUCH AS MANGO, BLUEBERRY, OR
EVEN BANANA. CITRUS FRUITS
WON'T WORK WELL BECAUSE
THE ACID WILL CAUSE THE DAIRY
TO CURDLE. IF YOU USE A FRESH
FRUIT PURÉE, INCREASE THE
COOK TIME TO 30 MINUTES.

Per Serving
Calories: 148; Fat: 4g;
Carbohydrates: 23g; Fiber: 1g;
Protein: 6g; Sodium: 61mg

Sometimes all you need are some simple ingredients to create a delicious and decadent dessert. This custard is the perfect example. With just a few ingredients and the fresh fruit of your choice, this custard is sure to become a favorite. What's more, it's also perfect to make ahead for parties and potlucks.

½ cup plain Greek yogurt

½ cup sweetened
condensed milk

½ teaspoon ground cinnamon

2 cups water

¼ cup chopped fruit or berries
of your choice, for garnish

1. **Prepare the custard.** In a heatproof bowl that fits inside the Instant Pot®, mix together the yogurt, condensed milk, and cinnamon. Tightly cover the bowl with aluminum foil.

2. **Pressure cook the custard.** Pour the water into the inner pot, and place the trivet inside. Place the bowl on the trivet, and lock the lid into place. Select Pressure Cook or Manual, and adjust the pressure to High and the time to 25 minutes. Make sure the steam release knob is in the sealed position. After cooking, naturally release the pressure.

3. **Chill the custard.** Unlock and remove the lid. Carefully remove the bowl. Let it cool at room temperature for 30 minutes, then refrigerate, covered, for 3 to 4 hours. Serve garnished with the fruits of your choice.

INDIAN-STYLE CARROT AND COCONUT KHEER

DAIRY-FREE, GLUTEN-FREE, NUT-FREE, VEGAN

SERVES 6

PREP AND FINISHING: 10 MINUTES, PLUS 10 MINUTES TO COOL

PRESSURE COOK:
15 MINUTES ON HIGH

RELEASE: NATURAL

SAUTÉ: 5 MINUTES

TOTAL TIME: 50 MINUTES

PAIR IT: PAIR THIS AS A DESSERT WITH THE VEGETABLE BIRYANI (PAGE 82) FOR A SCRUMPTIOUS MEAL.

Per Serving
Calories: 195; Fat: 10g;
Carbohydrates: 29g; Fiber: 2g;
Protein: 1g; Sodium: 27mg

Kheer, a sweet pudding, is an important feature of any festive Indian menu. The pudding is often made with rice, but I've seen it made with cracked wheat, rice vermicelli, tapioca pearls, and nuts and rice. My favorite is with carrot and coconut milk. The subtle sweetness of carrots is enhanced with the addition of brown sugar; the coconut milk adds creaminess. Kheer is often associated with Indian celebrations, but my version is a perfect dessert for any occasion.

3 carrots, peeled and cut into large chunks (about 1½ cups)

2 cups water

¾ cup cane sugar

3 whole cloves, crushed

2 cardamom seeds

1 cup full-fat coconut milk

1. Pressure cook the carrots. Place the carrots in the inner pot, and add the water. Lock the lid into place. Select Pressure Cook or Manual, and adjust the pressure to High and the time to 15 minutes. Make sure the steam release knob is in the sealed position. After cooking, naturally release the pressure.

2. Purée the carrots. Unlock and remove the lid. Drain the carrots, reserving 1 cup of the water. Let the carrots cool for 10 minutes. In a blender, combine the carrots and reserved cooking water. Purée until smooth.

3. Finish the kheer. Select Sauté. Once hot, add the carrot purée and sugar. Stir in the cloves and cardamom seeds, and simmer for 2 minutes or until the sugar has dissolved. Stir in the coconut milk, and simmer for another 3 minutes. Transfer to a serving bowl, and serve warm.

DULCE DE LECHE

GLUTEN-FREE, NUT-FREE

SERVES 4

PREP AND FINISHING: 5 MINUTES,
PLUS 30 MINUTES TO COOL

PRESSURE COOK:
45 MINUTES ON HIGH

RELEASE: NATURAL

TOTAL TIME: 1 HOUR 30 MINUTES

USE IT UP: ON RARE OCCASIONS
WHEN YOU HAVE LEFTOVERS,
USE THEM AS A TOPPING FOR ICE
CREAM, AS A DIP FOR APPLES,
OR AS A TOPPING FOR THE
APPLE-PEAR CRISP (PAGE 110).

Per Serving
Calories: 319; Fat: 9g;
Carbohydrates: 54g;
Fiber: 0g; Protein: 8g;
Sodium: 478mg

I always keep sweetened condensed milk in my pantry. It comes in handy for whipping up some quick desserts. This Dulce de Leche pudding is one of my favorites. Just two ingredients and minimal effort—it really can't get much easier. You're going to love the rich and creamy texture, and that right amount of sweetness.

1 (14-ounce) can sweetened condensed milk

2 cups water

1 teaspoon sea salt

Chopped almonds, for topping (optional)

Chopped chocolate, for topping (optional)

1. **Prepare the ramekins.** Evenly divide the condensed milk among four ramekins, three inches in diameter. Tightly cover each with aluminum foil.

2. **Pressure cook the Dulce de Leche.** Pour the water into the inner pot, and place the trivet inside. Place the ramekins on the trivet, stacking them if needed. Lock the lid into place. Select Pressure Cook or Manual, and adjust the pressure to High and the time to 45 minutes. Make sure the steam release knob is in the sealed position. After cooking, naturally release the pressure. Unlock and remove the lid. Carefully remove the ramekins. Remove the foil, and sprinkle with the sea salt. Let cool for 30 minutes before topping with chopped almonds and chocolate, if desired, and serving.

LEMON BUNDT CAKE

NUT-FREE

SERVES 6

PREP AND FINISHING: 15 MINUTES,
PLUS 30 MINUTES TO COOL

PRESSURE COOK:
30 MINUTES ON HIGH

RELEASE: NATURAL

TOTAL TIME: 1 HOUR 25 MINUTES

INGREDIENT TIP: INSTEAD
OF LEMONS, YOU CAN MAKE
THIS CAKE WITH ORANGE
JUICE AND ORANGE ZEST OR
A COMBINATION OF BOTH.

Per Serving
Calories: 417; Fat: 19g;
Carbohydrates: 56g;
Fiber: 1g; Protein: 7g;
Sodium: 279mg

I love citrus flavors in my dessert. They bring freshness that you don't find in other types of sweet treats. This soft and spongy lemon cake is one of my personal favorites. Here, the drizzled lemon frosting adds a touch of decadent sweetness to the cake.

1 cup plain Greek yogurt

¾ cup sugar

½ teaspoon baking soda

1¼ teaspoons baking powder

½ teaspoon kosher salt

1½ cups all-purpose flour

½ cup corn oil, plus more to grease the pan

1 tablespoon plus ½ teaspoon freshly squeezed lemon juice, divided

1½ teaspoons grated lemon zest

2 cups water

¼ cup confectioners' sugar

1. **Prepare the yogurt mix.** In a large bowl, whisk together the yogurt and sugar until the sugar is well dissolved. Stir in the baking soda, baking powder, and salt. Set aside for 5 minutes or until the mixture begins to bubble.

2. **Sift the flour.** Meanwhile, sift the flour into a medium bowl.

3. **Prepare the batter.** Whisk the yogurt mixture, then slowly whisk in the oil until fully incorporated. Stir in ½ teaspoon of lemon juice and the lemon zest. Add the sifted flour, and gently mix to form a smooth batter. Grease a Bundt cake pan with corn oil, and pour in the batter. Tap the pan twice on the counter to break any air pockets, and tightly cover with aluminum foil.

→

4. Pressure cook the cake. Pour the water into the inner pot, and place the trivet inside. Place the pan on the trivet, and lock the lid into place. Select Pressure Cook or Manual, and adjust the pressure to High and the time to 30 minutes. Make sure the steam release knob is in the sealed position. After cooking, naturally release the pressure.

5. Assemble the cake. Unlock and remove the lid. Remove the pan, and slowly remove the foil. Let the cake cool for at least 30 minutes. Run the knife along the edge of the pan, and invert the cake onto a plate. In a small bowl, add the remaining 1 tablespoon of lemon juice to the confectioners' sugar and mix thoroughly. Drizzle the glaze on top of the cake and serve.

BROWNIES

NUT-FREE

SERVES 6

PREP AND FINISHING:
10 MINUTES, PLUS AT LEAST
30 MINUTES TO COOL

PRESSURE COOK:
35 MINUTES ON HIGH

RELEASE: NATURAL

TOTAL TIME: 1 HOUR 25 MINUTES

INGREDIENT TIP: COFFEE CAN
ADD DEPTH TO ANY CHOCOLATE
RECIPE. FOR THIS BROWNIE
RECIPE, ADD 1 TO 1½ TEASPOONS
OF INSTANT COFFEE GRANULES
ALONG WITH THE DRY
INGREDIENTS. COOK TIME AND
PRESSURE REMAIN THE SAME.

Per Serving
Calories: 228; Fat: 9g;
Carbohydrates: 35g;
Fiber: 2g; Protein: 4g;
Sodium: 744mg

I love a warm brownie with a sprinkle of sea salt. My husband loves his served with ice cream. And my son prefers his covered in chocolate syrup. However you like your brownie, this one will surely meet your chocolate requirements. Remember, brownies cooked in an Instant Pot® are more cakelike than brownies baked in a conventional oven. But, I promise, the chocolatey goodness is just as satisfying.

1 cup all-purpose flour

¼ cup cocoa powder

¾ cup confectioners' sugar

1 teaspoon baking powder

½ teaspoon baking soda

¼ cup plain Greek yogurt

½ cup milk

3 tablespoons plus 1 teaspoon corn oil, divided

2 cups water

2 teaspoons sea salt

1. Prepare the dry ingredients. In a large bowl, sift together the flour, cocoa powder, and sugar. Add the baking powder and baking soda, and mix to combine.

2. Prepare the wet ingredients. In a medium bowl, whisk together the yogurt, milk, and 3 tablespoons of oil.

3. Prepare the batter. Little by little, add the wet ingredients to the dry ingredients, gently folding them together with each addition to form a smooth batter. Grease a springform pan with the remaining 1 teaspoon of oil. Pour the batter into the pan, and tightly cover with aluminum foil.

4. Pressure cook the Brownies. Pour the water into the inner pot, and place the trivet inside. Place the pan on the trivet, and lock the lid into place. Select Pressure Cook or Manual, adjusting the pressure to High and the time to 35 minutes. Make sure the steam release knob is in the sealed position. After cooking, naturally release the pressure. Unlock and remove the lid. Remove the pan, and remove the foil. Sprinkle the brownies with the sea salt, and let cool for at least 30 minutes. Gently remove from the pan, slice, and serve.

BANANA CAKE

SERVES 6

PREP AND FINISHING:
10 MINUTES, PLUS AT LEAST
30 MINUTES TO COOL

PRESSURE COOK:
30 MINUTES ON HIGH

RELEASE: NATURAL

TOTAL TIME: 1 HOUR 20 MINUTES

MAKE IT NUT-FREE: YOU
CAN SKIP THE NUTS AND ADD
CHOCOLATE CHIPS FOR AN
EVEN MORE DECADENT CAKE.

Per Serving
Calories: 497; Fat: 18g;
Carbohydrates: 79g;
Fiber: 2g; Protein: 5g;
Sodium: 192mg

I cannot have a dessert chapter without a banana recipe. Where dessert is concerned, when in doubt, go with bananas! This is a simple yet delicious Banana Cake made with pecans and walnuts. Wow your guests at your next gathering, and be prepared to share the recipe.

1½ cups all-purpose flour

1½ teaspoons baking powder

½ teaspoon baking soda

2 medium very ripe bananas

½ cup sugar

¼ cup milk

¼ cup corn oil, plus more to grease the pan

10 pecans, crushed, divided

10 walnuts, crushed, divided

2 cups water

1 cup vanilla cream cheese frosting

1. **Prepare the dry ingredients.** In a large bowl, sift together the flour, baking powder, and baking soda.

2. **Purée the bananas.** In a blender, purée the bananas until smooth. Set aside 1 cup of the purée.

3. **Prepare the wet ingredients.** In a large bowl, mix together the sugar, banana purée, milk, and oil.

4. **Prepare the batter.** Add the wet ingredients to the dry ingredients, and gently mix to form a smooth batter. Add 5 pecans and 5 walnuts to the batter, and gently fold them in. Grease a springform cake pan with some oil. Pour in the batter, and tap the pan twice on the counter to break any air pockets. Tightly cover the pan with aluminum foil.

5. Pressure cook the cake. Pour the water into the inner pot, and place the trivet inside. Place the cake on the trivet, and lock the lid into place. Select Pressure Cook or Manual, and adjust the pressure to High and the time to 30 minutes. Make sure the steam release knob is in the sealed position. After cooking, naturally release the pressure.

6. Decorate the cake. Unlock and remove the lid. Remove the cake pan and slowly remove the foil. Let the cake cool for at least 30 minutes. Release the cake from the springform pan. Frost the cake, and sprinkle the remaining pecans and walnuts on top. Slice and serve.

Instant Pot® Pressure Cooking Time Charts

The following charts provide estimated pressure cooking times for a number of vegetarian foods. Keep in mind that times may vary slightly, so you might want to cook foods for a minute or two less than suggested the first time you try them. Also, remember that the foods in these charts might have different cooking times and release methods when used in recipes alongside other ingredients and cooking liquids.

BEANS AND LEGUMES (WATER RATIO 1:2)

The following cook times and pressure levels all assume that you're cooking less than a pound of beans and legumes. Be sure to add a little oil to keep the foam down. If you are cooking more than 1 pound of beans and legumes, choose low pressure and increase the cooking time by a minute or two. The low pressure will reduce the chance of foaming, so there's no need to add any oil.

	Prep	Minutes Under Pressure	Pressure Level	Release
Black beans	Soaked overnight	8 to 10	High	Natural
Black-eyed peas	Soaked 4 hours	10	High	Natural for 10 minutes, then quick
Cannellini beans	Soaked overnight	15 to 20	High	Natural
Chickpeas	Soaked overnight	15 to 20	High	Natural
Fava beans	Soaked overnight	40	High	Natural
Kidney beans	Soaked overnight	15 to 20	High	Natural
Lentils, brown	Soaked 30 minutes	7 to 10	High	Natural
Lentils, green	Soaked 30 minutes	10 to 15	High	Natural
Lentils, red	Soaked 30 minutes	5	High	Natural
Lima beans	Soaked overnight	5	High	Natural for 10 minutes, then quick
Navy beans	Soaked overnight	12 to 15	High	Natural
Pinto beans	Soaked overnight	15 to 20	High	Natural
Yellow split peas	Soaked 10 minutes	10 to 15	High	Natural

GRAINS

Foaming is also an issue with grains. One way to prevent that from happening is to rinse your grains prior to cooking. Adding a little oil or butter will also do the trick.

	Minutes Under Pressure	Water Ratio	Pressure Level	Release
Barley	30	1:2.5	High	Natural
Bulgur wheat	2 to 4	1:1.25	High	Natural for 5 minutes, then quick
Couscous	3	1:1.25	High	Natural for 5 minutes, then quick
Farro	3	1:2	High	Natural for 5 minutes, then quick
Oats, rolled	5	1:3	High	Natural for 10 minutes, then quick
Oats, steel-cut	8 to 10	1:3	High	Natural for 10 minutes, then quick
Quinoa	8	1:1.5	High	Natural for 10 minutes, then quick
Rice, basmati	4	1:1.25	High	Natural for 3 minutes, then quick
Rice, brown	25	1:1.5 to 2	High	Natural
Rice, white	12	1:1.5 to 2	Low	Natural

VEGETABLES

The cooking method for all the following vegetables is steaming; if the vegetables are cooked directly in the liquid, the times may vary. Unless a shorter release time is indicated, let these vegetables naturally release for around 15 minutes, then quick release any remaining pressure.

	Prep	Minutes under Pressure	Pressure	Release
Artichokes, canned	Quartered	7	High	Quick
Asparagus	Edges trimmed	1	High	Quick
Beets	Whole	8	High	Quick
Broccoli	Florets	1	High	Quick
Brussels sprouts	Halved	1	High	Quick
Butternut Squash	Cut into chunks	6 to 7	High	Quick
Cabbage	Shredded	1	High	Quick
Carrots	Cut into chunks	5	High	Quick
Cauliflower	Cut into florets	1	Low	Quick
Cauliflower	Whole	6	High	Quick
Green beans	Cut in half or thirds	1	Low	Quick
Potatoes, large, russet (for mashing)	Quartered	8	High	Natural for 8 minutes, then quick
Potatoes, red	Whole if less than 1½" across, halved if larger	4	High	Quick
Spaghetti squash	Halved lengthwise	7	High	Quick
Sweet potatoes	Halved lengthwise	8	High	Natural

Measurement Conversions

VOLUME EQUIVALENTS (LIQUID)

U.S. Standard	U.S. Standard (ounces)	Metric (approximate)
2 tablespoons	1 fl. oz.	30 mL
¼ cup	2 fl. oz.	60 mL
½ cup	4 fl. oz.	120 mL
1 cup	8 fl. oz.	240 mL
1½ cups	12 fl. oz.	355 mL
2 cups or 1 pint	16 fl. oz.	475 mL
4 cups or 1 quart	32 fl. oz.	1 L
1 gallon	128 fl. oz.	4 L

OVEN TEMPERATURES

Fahrenheit (F)	Celsius (C) (approximate)
250º	120º
300º	150º
325º	165º
350º	180º
375º	190º
400º	200º
425º	220º
450º	230º

VOLUME EQUIVALENTS (DRY)

U.S. Standard	Metric (approximate)
⅛ teaspoon	0.5 mL
¼ teaspoon	1 mL
½ teaspoon	2 mL
¾ teaspoon	4 mL
1 teaspoon	5 mL
1 tablespoon	15 mL
¼ cup	59 mL
⅓ cup	79 mL
½ cup	118 mL
⅔ cup	156 mL
¾ cup	177 mL
1 cup	235 mL
2 cups or 1 pint	475 mL
3 cups	700 mL
4 cups or 1 quart	1 L

WEIGHT EQUIVALENTS

U.S. Standard	Metric (approximate)
½ ounce	15 g
1 ounce	30 g
2 ounces	60 g
4 ounces	115 g
8 ounces	225 g
12 ounces	340 g
16 ounces or 1 pound	455 g

Recipe Index

Index

Acknowledgments

First and foremost, I would like to thank God Almighty for giving me this great opportunity and the strength and ability to undertake this book and complete it.

To my dad, who is always watching me and blessing me from above.

To my mom, for introducing the art of cooking and teaching the same, and for all the love and support.

To my dear husband, without whom this journey would have been impossible. Thank you for believing in me and supporting me throughout this book journey. Without you, I would not be where I am today. I hope I've made you all proud.

To my son and my fur child, for adjusting their life to my crazy schedule. You guys are my source of strength.

I want to thank the editorial team of Callisto Media. Thank you for being so patient and helping me with recipe formats and all the edits.

Last but not least, I would like to thank all my friends, family, and readers for all of the love, support, and encouragement they have sent my way along this journey.

About the Author

Srividhya Gopalakrishnan is a software engineer and a passionate home cook and food blogger. As much as she loves to develop websites, she likes to develop new recipes, explore traditional foods, and research ingredients. She started her blog vidhyashomecooking.com in 2009 to share her family recipes and to record and revive authentic Indian food. Her blog contains more than 900 vegetarian and vegan recipes, including traditional Indian food, kid-friendly fusion food, eggless bakes, and Instant Pot® recipes from around the world. When she is not coding, cooking, clicking, and running after kids, she loves to read. She lives in the Bay Area of California with her husband, son, and four-legged fur child.

You can contact her at
vidhya@vidhyashomecooking.com
or on social media:
www.VidhyasHomeCooking.com
www.Instagram.com/VidhyasVegetarianKitchen/
www.Facebook.com/VidhyasVegetarianKitchen/

CPSIA information can be obtained
at www.ICGtesting.com
Printed in the USA
JSHW020904031120
9208JS00001B/1